Precious Deborah, I want you to

PICTURE
Perfect

God's Very Best For Your Life!

From Rob

Prov. 23-7

DR. ROB SPINA

Picture Perfect
Envision The Life God Designed For You
Dr. Rob Spina
Hope Unlimited Church
2780 S. Peck Rd. Monrovia, CA 91016
626-574-5044 | www.thehopeuc.com
Religion-Self Help
ISBN- 978-1-4951-2171-5

This book is available at quantity discounts for bulk purchase.

Special Note: The PICTURE PERFECT book is designed to provide the reader with information and motivation. It is sold with the understanding that the author or publisher is not engaged to render any type of psychological, medical, legal, financial, or any other kind of professional advice. This book is designed to educate the reader, showing what others have accomplished and God has promised in the Bible. Your individual results may vary and are solely the reader's responsibility. (22013a)

Table of Contents

Introduction............5

Chapter 1 - Let's Get On The Same Page............13

Chapter 2 - My Story - Why Carry The Weight?........19

Chapter 3 - Killing your Monsters............31

Chapter 4 - Why Do You Do What You Do?............43

Chapter 5 - Here's The Thing!............57

Chapter 6 - SEE The Good!............65

Chapter 7 - IN-VISION Your Success............73

Chapter 8 - What's Your Issue?............91

Chapter 9 - Close Your Eyes and Visualize!............105

Chapter 10 - Broadcast, Project, and
Radiate What You Desire............115

Chapter 11 - Jacob's Picture Produced............121

Chapter 12 - The Nuts and Bolts............129

Chapter 13 - Thought Cash-Does It Really Exist?..137

Chapter 14 - Breaking Your Self-Imposed
Limitations............153

Chapter 15 - If It's Alive - It's Meant To Thrive!........159

Chapter 16 - God Wants YOU Rightly Rich!...........167

Chapter 17 - Don't Ask God For Small Things -
    Thinking Small is Easier....................185

Chapter 18 - The Man Who IN-VISIONed
    the Future...191

Chapter 19 - The Flight Simulator of Your Mind.....203

Chapter 20 - Living With an Attitude of Gratitude.. 209

Chapter 21 - Lincoln Logs & Legos.......................217

Chapter 22 - Einstein Explains Hebrews 11.......... 231

Chapter 23 - God's Businessman...........................245

Chapter 24 - The Super Bowl of Your Life!............255

Introduction

The purpose of my ministry is all about change. There is a deep desire within me to see people from all walks of life come to a place of real, lasting, and beneficial change.

Get ready! This book's purpose is about empowering and revolutionizing your life!

I want to help you take a fresh look and get a new perspective concerning those areas of your life you've tried unsuccessfully to change. So many of us have tried to use our own willpower and dogged determination to change some important aspects of our lives. Most have found that over the years we have had little or no success.

Some of the areas we might have wanted to change could be things like improving our health, becoming more disciplined, diligent, or caring, creating more money, participating in a more meaningful life, or getting rid of any number of bad habits. Whatever it is in your life that you've wanted to change, you may have realized some measure of success, albeit for a limited period of time. But like most of us, you've inevitably relapsed somewhere along the line and found yourself back living the way you were previously living.

So many times in my past I found myself struggling to make the necessary changes and, for that reason, just barely *surviving*, not *thriving* as God intends. That's all about to change for you!

God Has Something Better For You!

We should know that God wants better for us and has better for us; we should also know that God is not only able to help us and bless us, but He is *WILLING* to help us and bless us. So what's the problem?

That's why I've written this book, to address the problem and show you the God-given way to conquer it, once and for all.

The challenges that lie ahead will require some major shifts in your thinking, but that's a good thing because if the way you had previously thought had gotten you what you wanted and desired, there'd be no need for change.

How many of us grew up thinking about becoming

a doctor, lawyer, police officer, astronaut or one of a thousand other professions? Did you grow up seeing yourself successfully operating on a patient, arguing and winning a case in court, speeding down the highway chasing and capturing the bad guys, or gliding through space?

As a child, it was easy for me to use my imagination. I'd lay on the grass, look up at the sky, and allow my imagination to soar. Unfortunately, somewhere along the way, I quit imagining and started accepting my circumstances as my reality, my lot in life. Actually, I quit using that powerful, God given tool that I now call the ability to *"IN-VISION."*

As I analyze what happened, I can see that I stopped sending myself fabulous and amazing mental pictures about what was possible for me; I started to look only at the pictures of what *"I can't be,"* what *"I can't do,"* and what *"I can't have."* I started looking at, and accepting, the small and limiting life that my circumstances presented to me. These pictures screamed that they were my reality, and up until recently, I believed them.

It's Time to IN-VISION a New You

Let me be bold and say that it's time to start *"IN-*

VISIONing" a new you. It's time to *"IN-VISION"* a new and amazing life. It's time to finally realize and experience that which you have dreamed about and desired for so long.

What an "IN-VISION" Really Is

An *"IN-VISION"* is all about getting a *PICTURE* on the inside of you, clearly showing you what you want to be, where you want to go, what you want to do, and what you want to have.

To *"IN-VISION"* is to have a picture, a mental photograph if you will, of where you want your finances to be, the way you'd like your relationships to develop, the kind of job or career you desire, or what you'd like to do for your family, friends, church and yourself.

An *"IN-VISION"* is almost like a spiritual blueprint that you will use to create your future and by which you will order your life. The goal will be to focus on what you magnificently *"IN-VISION"* and believe God while you think and work towards it with the determined confidence that you will certainly experience everything you have envisioned.

If Your Dreams Have Failed – Dream Bigger!

INTRODUCTION

This book is all about materializing your dreams and experiencing the desires of your heart. But before we begin, before we get into the actual lessons themselves, I want to challenge you to let go of the disappointments and failures of the past; start dreaming big and believing in the future the same way you did as a child!

I can hear some of you saying it under your breath right now, "Yeah, right! It's too late, Pastor Rob! Reality has already set in!" To that I'd say, "Whose reality?" You're probably thinking about Your Reality, based upon your past disappointments, letdowns, failures, and experiences, all of which did not match your desires.

Reality is What God Says Not What Circumstances Say

From this point forward, when we talk about reality, let's talk about God's Reality which is based upon His power to change yours. Reality, for us, will be about God's creative nature and His power to put His Super on your Natural and His Extra on your Ordinary, making your life supernatural and extraordinary!

Allow me to share a Bible story that explains what I mean when I say, *"IN-VISION."* Let's pick up the story about Jesus walking through a great crowd of people, from Mark 5:25-29.

"And a woman was there who had been subject to bleeding for twelve years. She had suffered a great deal under the care of many doctors and had spent all she had, yet instead of getting better she grew worse. When she heard about Jesus, she came up behind him in the crowd and touched his cloak, because she thought, 'If I just touch his clothes, I will be healed.' Immediately her bleeding stopped and she felt in her body that she was freed from her suffering."

The way this is rendered in the Greek gives us the idea that she *KEPT SAYING* over and over and over to herself, *"If I but just touch the hem of his garment, I WILL be healed."*

This woman had a mental photograph, an *"IN-VISION"* of what she wanted. She could picture in her mind that in the moment she touched Jesus' cloak, in the moment she reached up and grabbed the hem of His garment, healing power would flow from Jesus into her body and she would be gloriously healed of her disease.

She vividly *"IN-VISIONed,"* herself being healed and fully expected what she had been *"IN-VISIONing"* to actually happen. She *SAW* herself healed, in her mind, well before she saw healing manifest in her body. I will share with you how to use the exact same principle to receive everything you desire from God and life.

This woman's healing occurred just as she had *"IN-VISIONed."* When she grabbed the garment of Jesus, she experienced what she had *PICTURED* in her mind and received what she believed God for. That's how it will work for you, also!

In reality, she simply acted-out and received what she had already previously seen in her *"IN-VISION."* You might call her picture a *"Seed Thought"* or a *"Thought Seed"* because, like a seed, God designed us in such a way that the *mental pictures* at which we look often, in our mind, will grow and develop until they produce a perfect replication of what we have seen in our mind, in our actual experience.

This is what I want for you; I want for you to establish exactly who and what you want to become, what you want to do and experience in life, and what you want to have; then I want you to *VIVIDLY* begin to *"IN-VISION"* it.

The clarity of your picture, and the frequency with which you look at it, will put you on a path to receiving what you *"IN-VISION."* Because the bleeding woman continually said, *"When I touch the hem of his garment, I will be healed,"* we know for sure that she was sharpening the focus and vividness of the picture she was creating.

Our primary goal is all about getting the picture of what you desire from God and life deep within you, about *SEEING* it over and over and over again, and about watching its manifestation. Dig into the principles found in this book, put them into practice, and they will help you become more, do more, and have more than you ever thought possible.

**This Book Will Help You Succeed!
"IN-VISION" That!**

CHAPTER 1
Let's Get On The Same Page

From the get-go, I want us to be on the same page when I refer to "IN-VISION," because that's what this book is all about. Obviously, the base word for our study is "ENVISION" which means to *Imagine a future possibility, or to visualize.*

For this book, I have created a word that includes ENVISION, but is even stronger, and I trust will soon become one of the most important and meaningful words in your vocabulary.

The word I will be using is "IN-VISION." IN-VISION is made up of two words: *"IN"* talks about something internal, something inside you; *"VISION"* means something that you mentally *SEE* in a mental *PICTURE*.

We might say that your physical eyes see OUT-

VISION (things that are outside of you) but your mind sees *IN-VISION*.

To "IN-VISION" is to have a mental photograph of where you want your finances to be, the way you'd like your relationships to develop, what kind of job or career you desire, or what you'd like to do for your family, friends, church, and self.

An "IN-VISION" is all about getting a *picture* on the inside of you showing you what you want to be, where you want to go, what you want to do, or what you want to have.

This subject of *IN-VISIONing* is about changing the way you think and changing both the still and moving *pictures* you allow yourself to *view* over and over again in your mind. It's about meditating upon, pondering and staying focused on what God has promised you and what you'd really like out of life.

The Pictures From Radio Are Better Than the Pictures From Television

Understanding that we really do see in *PICTURES*, I thought you would enjoy the following little bit of history, a true story:

Television was gaining a foothold in Germany,

Britain, and France in the 1940s. Between 1947 and 1955, *Television* finally began to catch on in the United States. At that time, the wealthy and many upper-middle-class families purchased their first Television set. They would invite their friends over to experience this mind-boggling new discovery called, "Television."

Appliance stores would advertise the amazing *Television* by turning it on and having it face the display windows at night, so that a passersby could stand on the sidewalk and watch moving pictures from a wooden box. In those days, it always drew a crowd.

From the early 1900s to the mid-fifties, families would primarily use *radio* as their source of family entertainment. It seemed that every American household owned a radio. Every family member would gather around the *radio* at a certain time during the week to listen to their favorite broadcast.

Actors and entertainers would come together at radio stations and create stories, skits, plays, comedy, and dramas that were acted out *vocally*, and broadcast into the homes across America.

Radio featured detective stories about Sherlock Holmes, suspense with The Avenger, Charlie Chan, and Superman, westerns featuring Gunsmoke and Hop-along Cassidy, and comedy, starring celebrities such as Groucho Marx, Amos and Andy, and Bob

Hope. Radio provided entertainment for everyone.

It was in this setting that a father came home excited to tell his family that he had a marvelous treat for them. They had been invited to a friend's house that night to watch *Television* for their very first time.

After arriving back home from an enjoyable evening and a new experience, the father asked his eight-year-old daughter, "How did you like watching Television, honey?" To this the daughter replied, "It was wonderful daddy, but the *pictures* were not nearly as nice as the ones from radio."

It seems that the child's *imagination* painted a much more vivid *PICTURE* in her mind listening to the radio than the black-and-white television was capable of conveying.

IN-VISION Means to Send Yourself a Mental Picture

Webster's Dictionary says that the word, "Envision," means, "To send a *picture* to oneself." Most people fail because they only *send themselves* negative mental pictures and talk to themselves about their limitations and not about their possibilities. They review the negative pictures that they have envisioned (or sent to themselves) often, and talk to themselves continually about the fears that those pictures have portrayed.

I will show you how to overcome this debilitating habit and how to receive the good things in life that God has intended for you to experience. In this study, we are going to learn how to send ourselves powerful and godly *MENTAL PICTURES* that will start producing amazing happiness, success, and prosperity in our lives.

The creative power of *IN-VISION* may be explained this way: *I attract into my life the mirror image experience of the Mental Pictures to which I give my attention, energy, and focus, whether positive or negative.*

I would highly encourage you to memorize the above paragraph!

When you constantly expect that which you persistently *IN-VISION*, your ability to attract what you are *SEEING* becomes irresistible. Your mind really is like a magnet and attracts whatever corresponds to the *Mental Pictures* you use most often. You are a living magnet; you attract into your life the people, situations, and circumstances that are in harmony with what you think, picture, believe, and say.

Our ultimate goal: The ultimate goal is to fill our mind with the Word of God, what He said, and what He promised, so that we stop thinking about and creating mental pictures of insufficiency, lack, conflict, sickness, failure, and what we don't want to experience. We want to get to the place that we only think about and create mental pictures of what we do want and what God has promised.

CHAPTER 2
My Story – Why Carry The Weight?

I've been in the Ministry for over thirty-four years and most of that time has been spent behind a desk. Being in the ministry full-time doesn't require much manual labor except for getting up and walking to someone else's office and then, only to sit back down and have a conversation.

Multiplying all this lack of physical labor over the course of decades, you can see how easy it was for me to come to a point in my life where I had gained so much weight that I was tipping the scales in the three hundred and ninety pound neighborhood. If you think about it, that's a pretty exclusive neighborhood! So, each and every time I had to get up from my desk I was carrying quite a lot of weight, and boy, was it a strain.

I realized I had to get a new *IN-VISION* of a new me. I knew I had to create a new *MENTAL PICTURE* of the me I wanted to be. The *PICTURE* that I had inside of me, I had been carrying all of my life. It was one that said to me, "You'll always be a big guy and the sad, unchangeable fact is that you'll only get bigger from here."

The image I had of myself wasn't a picture I liked, but it was the only one I had and I had been looking at it every day, faithfully, for years. When you're at a point in your life that you can only see yourself in one position or pose, it's easy to understand why you stay the same. In fact, in this study, we are going to discover that we do everything in our power to cause our actual circumstances to perfectly match the *PICTURE* we have on the inside of us.

It's not that a multitude of diets weren't presented to me; they were, but none of them would work until I could *IN-VISION* myself thinner, healthier, and happier. I discovered that my primary goal was not to work on eating less, but first of all, to work on what I was *THINKING* and *PICTURING* in my mind.

**Once the Vision Changes,
So Does the Place of Arrival**

Once I had the proper *"IN-VISION,"* most any of the diets would work; but with an improper vision, *NO* diet would work. Understand this principle: once the mental vision or picture you have inside of you changes, so does the place of arrival. What do I mean by the place of arrival?

Well, imagine it like this: let's say you've bought an airline ticket to fly from L.A. to New York. So, the day of your journey, you arrive at the airport on time, check in for your flight, go through the aggravation of security, board the plane, and after a lengthy delay, the plane takes off. Finally, you settle into your seat, read a book, watch some inflight entertainment, daydream about visiting the Empire State Building or the Statue of Liberty, and before you know it, the pilot announces you'll soon be landing.

The plane lands, everyone disembarks, and as you walk through the terminal, you look out the window and realize that you are back in Los Angeles, the very place you started! I know this illustration may seem silly, and you may be thinking, "If I bought a ticket from an airline to go to New York, I'd darn well better get there." I agree!

When it comes to my weight, I can recount many times where I've paid for a ticket "to New York, from L.A.," only to end up back in "Los Angeles" again.

Ultimately, I wanted to end up in a skinnier pair of pants. So why, after much effort, sacrifice, and expense, would I end up as heavy or heavier than I was before?

My experience can be compared to the guy who left Los Angeles, expecting to end up in New York, only to end up in Los Angeles again. Here's how it works and here's how we turn out just like that guy. If the plane in which he flies is *PROGRAMED* to fly to Texas, to turn around, and then to come back to L.A., then that's exactly what it will do, every time!

In my case, my mental programing only allowed me to draw from the database of photographs and information that was within me. Every picture that I had stored within me only showed me as grossly overweight, and therefore, I was only capable of going in circles, as far as my diet and weight were concerned.

My desired destination always seemed just out of reach. Unfortunately, my actual destination always ended up being the same place I had started.

What about you? What database of photographs and information causes you to constantly go around in circles in certain areas of your life?

I'm going to show you how to replace that database of photographs and information with powerful new photographs and information, leading you to the destination God desires for you to experience.

A Truth That Will Change Your Life!

Meditate on this truth: Whatever photographs and information it is that you've allowed to be downloaded into your database... know this... that's all you will ever be capable of becoming, doing or having.

Are you beginning to see how important it is to get a new *"IN-VISION?"* A new *IN-VISION* is the only way your circumstances and destination will ever change.

One particular day (more than likely after a doctor's poor report), I said to myself that I just couldn't remain the same. Something had to change. However, I couldn't *PICTURE* myself any different than I had always been.

You see, for me, at fifty-two years of age, I had never experienced a normal weight. *"Normal"* for me was being overweight. The picture that I had sent to myself and viewed daily for almost fifty years convinced me that being overweight was how I was *supposed* to be. That was me. That was who I was.

It's funny how we can believe things and trust things to be true, when in fact, they are not true at all.

Repetition is a great convincer.

If, from the time you were a baby, you were constantly told and taught that the world was flat, you would believe it.

Understanding this important principle from God's Word is crucial for your success and development: *"For as a man thinks in his heart, so is he" (Proverbs 23:7).*

I realized that I could think many things about myself that I deemed to be the truth, but just weren't. It did not matter if it was the truth. All that mattered was that I believed it to be true.

The PRMS Translation of Proverbs 23:7 is rendered, *"As people picture their lives, the positive or negative things they see, can't help but be reproduced in their lives."*

I Was Only Seeing What I Was

I certainly did not believe that God wanted me to be overweight, but I just couldn't *SEE* myself any different. The only *Mental Picture* I had to look at my entire life was an overweight me. That picture was reinforced so many times that it was all that I was capable of seeing.

The *mental picture* that I had of myself was indelibly etched in my mind. It was like a video track that just kept playing over and over again in my mind. Realizing the only view I had of myself was that of being overweight, I thought, "I'm going to need to change my point of view. I need to change the portrait I have been seeing of myself."

Previously, up until this point in my life, I would have had to actually have been at a normal weight to believe I could ever be at a normal weight. But that's not faith! Faith believes before the manifestation of what it desires appears and before it physically *SEES* the manifestation; otherwise, it's not really faith.

So, understanding the principal of believing it before I could physically see it, I said, "I will now begin to see myself through the eyes of my faith at two hundred and sixteen pounds." That seemed awfully challenging and weird to me when I was almost one hundred and eighty pounds heavier, but nonetheless, I began to *picture* myself at that weight.

Wow! I'm Almost There

I'm so happy to report that at the writing of this book I've only got about forty pounds, or so, to go. Because

I said, "Or so," you might be asking, "Don't you know exactly how much you need to lose?" Actually, no, I don't. I've never been there, so I'm not exactly sure what my ideal weight will be, but I do know that it will be a place where, for the first time in my life, I can say that I'm at a normal weight.

Catch the "IN-VISION"

Simply put, I had to send myself new *PICTURES* and *"IN-VISION"* where I wanted to be, not just physically, but spiritually, financially, and in so many other areas of my life. I literally started sending myself mental *PICTURES* of who I wanted to be, what I wanted to do and have.

Today, there are far too many Christians who are overweight. What I mean by that is that they are carrying weights from their past that puts a strain and drain on them. Know that without a doubt, the wrong portraits that have been painted or the incorrect images that have been sculpted in your past have created your present. These weights do drain you and they do put a strain on you.

But God commands us to *"lay aside every weight"* (Hebrews 12:1). In context, this verse tells us to lay aside every weight, and the sin that so easily besets us. It's important for us to realize that the word "weight" here is not speaking of sin. Rather, a weight is something that slows us down or hinders our progress.

Like a father who carries a picture in his wallet of his family, some of you are carrying pictures in your mind of a past betrayal, a poor self-image, some heinous sin, failure, or disappointment; maybe you carry a picture of not living up to the expectations of others, yourself, or God.

These types of vivid and negative images work against you every day, in every way! They are detrimental to your spiritual, physical, financial, mental, and social life. These negative pictures stop you from being all that God has intended you to be. The negative pictures have become like a blueprint by which you order your life.

It should be clear by now that it's time to lose the weight, both the physical and mental weight you have been carrying. It's time to SEE yourself freed from the negative mental images that have contributed to a poor self image; allow God's positive images of you to develop fully on the inside and outside of you.

Now, take a moment to stop and picture in your mind what the Father has been speaking in your spirit. Picture what you know God has promised you in His

Word, even though you haven't yet seen it manifest in your life.

Picture yourself with your desire fully manifested and picture yourself enjoying it to the fullest. In whatever area, no matter how far off or impossible it may seem, your faith becomes your reality, the title-deed or pink-slip, proving that you legally own that which you're believing God has and will provide (Hebrews 11:1).

Another way to put it is like this: your faith (that which you *IN-VISION* and believe) becomes your focus. Your focus becomes clearer and clearer as you continually *SEE* yourself in possession of that which you believe you have received from God. Eventually, you will come to that place of *EXPERIENCING* what you've been *SEEING* from the moment you got a new *IN-VISION*.

My precious friends, whatever weight you've been carrying, let go of it and allow the grace of God that has come through Christ Jesus to set you completely free. You see, grace says, "You are clean. You are accepted in God. You are loved. YOU are a new person in Christ, regardless of your past, how you feel, or the negative pictures you have looked at for so long."

Grace says that you can stand before God without a sense of condemnation, without a sense of guilt, without a sense of shame, without a sense of rejection, without a sense of inferiority, and without a sense of fear! You HAVE perfect right-standing with God by the redemptive work of Jesus Christ, by grace and through faith (Ephesians 2:8-9).

Sin is not an issue any longer. That's been dealt with by Jesus Christ. Your performance (good or bad) is not an issue. Your Heavenly Father only looks at the performance of Jesus. You are in Christ, He is in you and you are a child of God.

Know this: like every good and gracious Father, God's desire is that you lose the weight that's been restricting your progress and happiness, the weight that has kept you from enjoying the *life more abundantly* that Jesus promised and provided (John 10:10).

CHAPTER 3
Killing Your Monsters

Johns Hopkins Medical Center and the *Mayo Clinic* have agreed that as much as seventy percent of their outpatient care is involved in treating patients whose illnesses were caused by psychosomatic reasons.

The term "psychosomatic" speaks of a physical illness or other negative physical conditions caused or aggravated by a mental factor such as internal conflict, stress, or worry. That term is also used relating to the interaction of mind and body. In other words, thinking improperly.

God told us two thousand years ago that our thinking affects our health. He basically said we would both prosper and be in good health if we could keep our mind thinking about prosperous, healthy, and beneficial things (3 John 2).

An Amazing True Story About Visualization

Some years ago I watched a very interesting documentary on *The Public Broadcast Network* (PBN) having to do with the effects *VISUALIZATION* has on cancer treatment. At first, the program was very heart-wrenching as it featured a six-year-old boy in the final stages of cancer. By the end of the show, I was praising Jesus.

The program started by showing young Matthew in a hospital room hooked up to monitors and tubes. The chemotherapy regiment they had put him through had depleted his bodies' strength and vigor, stolen his appetite, turned his skin pale gray, and caused all of his hair to fall out. Matthew looked like a skeleton with skin draped over his bones. The first sight of the poor child tore me up and made me weep.

Sitting in the room with him was his mother and father. They were engaging him in a conversation unrelated to his illness and it was quickly apparent that Matthew was a very bright young boy. The next scene in the documentary showed his doctor consulting the parents and explaining that all medical hope for their son's recovery was gone. He was in the final stage of brain cancer. However, the doctor said they weren't giving up.

The doctor's plan was to put Matthew in a new clinical study that the hospital was helping to conduct. It involved pairing Matthew with a child psychologist who had been getting amazing results utilizing *Visualization* to help enhance recovery. With no hope of recovery, medically speaking, the parents agreed to faithfully participate in the process.

Their doctor introduced them to the psychologist. The psychologist explained to the parents and then later to Matthew, what they were going to be doing was based on the medical discovery that your body and mind are connected. (As God said in 3 John 2.) The psychologist stated they would be using a technique called *Visualization*, a technique he also called *Guided Imagery* or *Creative Visualization*, to help Matthew.

At the time of this program, numerous studies had already supported the benefits of *Visualization*. It had already proven effective in treating a variety of conditions from asthma and anxiety to insomnia and fibromyalgia.

The idea was by providing positive *Mental Pictures*, creative imagery, and positive self-suggestion, visualization can change emotions that subsequently have a physical effect on the body. In other words, they were going to train a six-year-old how to *IN-VISION* something vastly different from what he was experiencing.

They were going to do this by creating a detailed schema of what they desired for Matthew and have him *IN-VISION* it over and over again, using all of his senses, in an effort to cause his mind to positively affect his body.

The Process of Matthew's Miracle

The next scene in the program showed the psychologist sitting on a carpeted floor somewhere in the hospital playing blocks with Matthew, then Matthew and the psychologist sitting at a short table talking and joking around.

At one point Matthew was asked if he liked to draw and color. He responded that he did. The doctor then asked him to draw his family and his house. The drawing Matthew made was with crayons and looked like a typical six-year-old drawing. The psychologist acted very excited about what Matthew had drawn. He said by drawing pictures and thinking about the pictures, they were going to conquer cancer, together.

The psychologist asked Matthew what he thought about when he *Pictured* the cancer in his body. Matthew answered, "I Picture it as a monster on the inside of me making me hurt." The doctor told Matthew to draw a picture of himself with the monster standing next to him. Matthew did. In the picture, Matthew was about the height of a third of the piece of paper. The monster he drew standing next to him was as tall as the full sheet of paper.

Matthew drew himself as a stick boy and the monster was a big, thick, and powerful brute. In perspective, Matthew was a three or four-inch tall stick boy, and the monster was eleven inches tall, large and bulky.

The drawing showed the doctor how Matthew viewed himself compared to his problem. The drawing let the doctor know what Matthew was *IN-VISIONing*.

The doctor instructed Matthew to draw a picture of himself with a special gun in his hand. He was told to draw a picture of the monster, but this time to draw nostrils or noses all over the monster. Matthew put two small black circles together all over the face and chest of the monster, representing many nostrils. Matthew was told to put even more nostrils and noses all over the monster until his body was totally covered with nostrils. He was then told that his special gun could shoot sticky green goo that was capable of plugging up the nostrils of the monster, making it difficult for the monster to breathe.

Matthew's assignment was to draw himself shooting the monster with sticky green goo and plugging up some of the monsters nostrils. Matthew had to make this same drawing several times every day. For the rest of the day he had to think about what his drawing would look like tomorrow.

In addition to this, he and his parents had to *Visualize* the fact that the monster was getting smaller and weaker because he couldn't breathe and that Matthew was getting bigger and stronger as the monster got smaller. Each day, he was supposed to draw the monster being more and more covered with sticky green goo.

At first, it was just the monster's face that was covered with sticky green goo, then his shoulders, his stomach, one arm, and so forth. Every day Matthew drew the monster, it looked a little bit smaller (maybe half an inch smaller) and the drawing of himself looked a little bit bigger.

They were not trying to rush the process because the psychologist knew it would take time for Matthew to truly and vividly Picture what was happening. The goal was for Matthew's Mental Image, what he was

IN-VISIONing, to become very sharp and defined. The psychologist hoped for what we would call today a *"High Resolution Picture."*

Pretty soon, the sticky green-goo-covered monster and Matthew looked about the same size on the paper. Every time Matthew drew the monster, he drew more and more of its nostrils covered with goo, making it even harder for the monster to breathe. Eventually, after several weeks, the monster was smaller than Matthew. As they continued with this discipline of drawing and visualizing, Matthew became eleven inches tall and the monster only four inches tall on paper, reflecting how Matthew Pictured the situation in his mind.

Matthew was to draw what he *SAW*. Remember, the drawing reflected how Matthew, in his mind, compared himself with the monster. Matthew's drawings now indicated that in his thinking, the monster was dying and Matthew was getting stronger. Amazingly, Matthew's health had improved so much that he would soon be released from the hospital. The doctors and scientists running the study videotaped the progress every day. Matthew's health showed an obvious and definite improvement.

One More Exercise

Before the monster completely died from suffocation caused by Matthew's sticky green goo gun, Matthew was given another mental exercise that he had to perform every night before he went to sleep. He had to agree to continue the new exercise for years, if necessary.

Matthew had to close his eyes and *IN-VISION* himself turning into a clean, white washcloth. Any anger, fear, hurt feelings, or frustration Matthew experienced during that day were to be visualized as dirty spots on the clean, white washcloth.

In his mind, Matthew had to view himself as a clean white washcloth with whatever dirty spots he picked up during the day. He then had to *IN-VISION* himself being dunked in pure, refreshing water and wrung-out, to Visualize all the dirt leaving his life as the water was squeezed out of the cloth.

Mathew also had to see himself as perfectly happy and clean as he let go of anything that had offended him, troubled him, or worried him during the day. The purpose of the exercise: Matthew had to purge himself every night of any bad feelings, disharmony, or worries that could contribute to ill health.

Fast Forward Four Years

At the end of the broadcast they showed an unrecognizable ten or eleven-year-old boy, healthy and strong, playing on the local Little League team. It was Matthew! The commentator explained that Matthew had continued to draw himself squirting the monster with sticky green goo until the monster finally vanished. He had also continued drawing himself until he no longer looked like a stick person, but a strong, healthy boy.

In addition to this, Matthew still mentally purged himself of any bad feelings before he went to sleep at night, *IN-VISIONing* himself happy and healthy.

For him, this powerful principle of *IN-VISIONing* was simply sending himself a *MENTAL PICTURE* of what he wanted his physical condition to be; he then looked at this mental picture frequently, all the time improving the picture as he brought it more and more into focus. As he did this exercise, it was critical that he held fast to the firm belief that he would soon experience what his mental picture had shown him.

You can do the same! You can experience *Picture Perfect Health!*

How this Process Applies to You

Any new *Picture* or program you wish to indelibly

imprint on your subconscious mind must be nurtured. Therefore, it is necessary to repeat the desired condition often, until the subconscious mind totally accepts it. Even after accepted, the image and program should repeat periodically to ensure that it remains the dominant Picture and intention in your mind.

The plan they used with Matthew involved slowly and surely developing the image of the cancer dying and Matthew getting stronger. Let me emphasize that Matthew and his parents didn't agree to "try" to visualize the monster dying or dabble with this new visualization concept.

Matthew and his parents committed to work the program. They didn't commit to "try;" they committed to do it wholeheartedly, knowing that the connotation of try is to attempt to do something but not necessarily to succeed.

They worked the process of *IN-VISIONing* deliberately, faithfully, and diligently, because they knew life or death hung in the balance. As you can clearly see, Matthew's parents had to buy into and believe in the process, knowing if they didn't believe it would work, Matthew would have had no chance of recovery. It was not on again – off again, when they remembered, or when it proved convenient. *VISUALIZATION* was now their top priority and lifestyle.

The psychologist imprinted into the minds of Matthew's parents that their goal must be clearly defined and kept before their eyes every day, otherwise their Picture would become vague and blurred, morphing into something other than the desired result.

Matthew's parents came to understand that when Matthew's subconscious mind recognized and accepted the concept of the monster getting smaller, and himself getting healthier, that the mind would begin to send that message to his body. They came to discover that every thought or idea causes a physical reaction.

Thoughts Cause Physical Reactions

Suppose you have to give a speech or presentation, something completely out of your comfort zone. Perhaps you are called into the boss's office unexpectedly. Imagine you are a kid going up to bat in the bottom of the ninth inning, bases-loaded, the score tied, with two outs. The conditions I have just described certainly affect your body. Maybe it would even be hard to smile because your mind is telling you how difficult this will be, how bad the situation is, and how you will look if you fail.

Those thoughts manifest in the way you hold yourself, your facial expressions, shortness of breath, rapid heartbeat, nervous twitches, maybe even the shakes. Now, flip the script. What does you being blessed look like? Matthew and his parents had to *IN-VISION* (send themselves a Mental Picture of) what a healthy Matthew would look like; they had to do it over and over and over again! Until you specifically know what blessed, for you, will look like, it's hard to *Visualize* it and impossible to achieve it.

The psychologists instructed Matthew and his family to use all their senses during their Visualization to invoke as much emotion as they could and, with emotion, repetition, expectation of success, and a positive attitude, they would conquer cancer.

Are there "Monster's" in your life that need to be eliminated? This process of *VISUALIZATION* is a law that God put into motion at the beginning of creation and remains today. You can do the same thing that Matthew and his parents did! In addition to this, if there's anything in your life, that is super important for you to become or to materialize, I encourage you to follow Matthew's recipe. Beginning right now!

Picture Perfect Health!

CHAPTER 4
Why Do You Do What You Do?

Webster's Dictionary says that the word *Determined* is, *"The firm or fixed intention to achieve a desired end."* There is great power in making a decision and being firm about it. There is great power in having your attention fixed on what you desire, which is the God result.

Don't allow yourself to look at other *MENTAL PHOTOS* that portray wrong and unwanted results. You've done that for long enough; that didn't work.

Remember the woman with the issue of blood I talked about in the introduction of the book and how she kept *SEEING* herself touching the hem of Jesus' garment? She was willing to do whatever it took to touch the hem of Jesus' garment as she had *IN-*

VISIONed.

You see, she was really stepping out in faith. Jewish ceremonial law said it was unlawful for her to be around other people because her bleeding made her unclean. Her whole religious life, the entire paradigm of her life, was to obey the rules, even if those rules caused her demise.

How sad it would have been if the woman in our story had done things the way they'd always been done; she would have never been healed.

However, upon hearing about Jesus and His healing of all that were sick and oppressed of the devil, a *PICTURE* began to formulate in her mind. A picture that defied the guidelines, the rules, and the way other people believed and acted.

Her picture, the photo she constantly kept before her mind's eye, spoke to her, saying that Jesus had what she needed: healing, wholeness, and freedom from her infirmity.

It seems to me that there are many churches and well-meaning people who are determined to do things their own way or the way things have always been done, even if it kills them. What you must realize is, we've got to do things God's way in order to get God's results. Here's the painful rub. What you've been told is God's way, may not be God's way at all. Hence, the absence of God's manifestations and good results.

IN-VISIONing God's Word proving true in your case, is God's way. But many well-meaning believers refuse to get a new *IN-VISION*, because they can't possibly *SEE* or *IMAGINE* themselves doing things any different from the way they've always done them.

Why Do You Do What You've Been Doing?

Perhaps you heard about the young girl who asked her mom, "Mom, why do you cut off the last two inches of the ham before you put it in the pan?" Her mom responded, "I've always done it that way, but I'm not sure why; go ask your grandmother, I learned it from her." Her grandmother, upon hearing the same question, gave this reply, "I've always done it that way. I don't know why, but go ask your great-grandmother. She's the one that taught me and she'll know why."

Finally, the young girl went to her great-grandmother who responded to the same question with this answer: "The only reason I cut off two inches of the ham was because back in the old days I only had a small pan and the entire ham didn't fit in the pan. My daughter and your mother must have seen me cut the ham and thought it was for another reason. Back then, I always had to cook the two inches of ham that I cut off separately, at a later date."

Obviously, each succeeding generation believed that cutting two inches off of the ham somehow improved the flavor, when in reality, it was just wasting the ham and money.

Instead of wasting time, energy, finances, or anything of value on things that just don't work, let's be determined to get a new "IN-VISION" and change our future with beneficial things that do work! We do this by being fixed and focused on our desired destination, not a destination determined by anyone or anything else other than the desirable photographs we are sending ourselves.

Let's take a look at a story from Matthew 14:22. *"Immediately Jesus made the disciples get into the boat and go on ahead of him to the other side, while he dismissed the crowd."* The disciples had just been a part of the miracle of feeding thousands of people with a little boy's lunch of bread and fish and now Jesus tells them to go on ahead of Him across the lake to the other side.

Matthew 14:23-25 (NIV) *"After he had dismissed them, he went up on a mountainside by himself to pray. When evening came, he was there alone, but the boat was already a considerable distance from land, buffeted by the waves because the wind was against it. During the fourth watch of the night Jesus went out to them, walking on the lake."*

So here they are without Jesus in their boat. A wind has arisen that's beating them up. It's the fourth watch, meaning it's somewhere between three to six a.m. and it's dark.

Have you ever been in a similar situation? Maybe you were in an amazing service where people were being blessed and God was feeding you, speaking to you about where He wants you to be, and showing the *IN-VISION* He has for you.

During the meeting your faith and confidence level was high. Then you get home and find that you're in the same position the disciples were in: alone in the dark, getting beat up by thoughts crashing against your mind, telling you that you'll never get to the destination that an hour ago you saw with absolute clarity.

Where's Jesus to help? The reason the disciples were out in the middle of the lake facing adversity was because they did what Jesus had told them to do. They had taken His direction for their life.

Now remember, Jesus hadn't called them to go out and get beat up by a storm and drown. No, He told

Go Over to the Other Side

them to go to the other side. Look closely at this next statement and meditate upon the truth of what you read: "God will not tell you where to go, what to do, and to enjoy life, without giving you the ability to do it."

Jesus told His disciples to go to the other side; therefore, the power of God was present to help them accomplish what Jesus said. God's power is always present to help you accomplish anything He tells you to do or have.

Live in the Land of Courage, Faith and Victory

At one time in my life, there was a side of me that was constantly discouraged, constantly doubting, and constantly defeated. But there came a day when I knew that Jesus had said to me, "Go on over to the other side. Live in the land of courage, faith, and victory."

Let's get back to the story: *"When the disciples saw him walking on the lake, they were terrified. 'It's a ghost,' they said, and cried out in fear"* (Matthew 14:26 NIV). I think I would have been a little freaked out, too. Couldn't Jesus have shown up when the sun was up or borrowed someone's boat to get to His disciples? No, He walked to them on the water, in the dark.

So they're in the dark, they're alone, they're getting beat up, and now fear has entered their boat (because fear was first entertained in their minds). Fear said, "You won't make it. You are going to die!" In an attempt to stop your forward progress, fear conjures up a mental, high definition picture that shows you as already defeated, so why even try.

It's at this point that most people accept defeat, and therefore, don't even try to go forward. After all, what's the use? Matthew 14:27 *"But Jesus immediately said to them: 'Take courage! It is I. Don't be afraid.'"* The Greek definition for the words, *"Take Courage,"* means, *"To boldly exercise confidence."*

Did you notice that it said, "Take Courage?" This means courage is available to you, but you have to *TAKE IT*. Grab ahold of it, embrace it, and make it yours! I so love this! You have the *IN-VISION*, and yes, things have come against you to get you away from ever realizing the picture that is in you. However, Jesus is telling you right now to boldly exercise your confidence, because courage is yours for the taking and it's up to you.

Which picture will you meditate and focus on? The one that shows the wind and waves sinking your boat while you drown, or the photo that reminds you that Jesus said, *"Go on over to the other side?"*

Which Picture Will You Meditate and Focus On?

Matthew 14:28-29 *"'Lord, if it's you,' Peter replied, 'tell me to come to you on the water.'" 'Come,' he said. Then Peter got down out of the boat, walked on the water and came toward Jesus."*

Now the disciples are seeing Jesus in a way they'd never seen Him before. They'd seen Him do some amazing things, but now He's there defying the law of gravity and He's not *"SINKING."*

When You SEE Something Different, You GET Something Different

Allow me to say this to you as succinctly as I can. This is the day for you to begin seeing (picturing) Jesus doing things for you that you've never seen Him do before, so you can have, do, and experience things you've never had, done, or experienced before. *IN-VISION* that!

Notice that Jesus never said, "Yes Peter it's me." We know Peter didn't recognize Jesus by sight, and we know that Jesus never said, "It's me." So then, why did Peter get out of the boat? He got out of the boat because he had a relationship with Jesus and he recognized His voice. Don't you just love the boldness of Peter? I see this as Peter saying to Jesus, "If it's you, then I want to be where you are, doing what you're doing, and getting the same result that you're getting."

As an *IN-VISIONary*, I constantly *IN-VISION* myself being where Jesus would be, doing what He would do, and getting the results that He would get! I believe this is what Jesus was referring to when He said, *"The works that I do, shall you do also"* (John 14:12).

What am I saying? Simply this: Jesus blessed, Jesus healed, Jesus prospered, Jesus loved, Jesus grew in wisdom, Jesus forgave, Jesus met needs, and Jesus went about correcting all the wrong beliefs that so many people heard about Him and His Father.

Today I can say that I am seeing Jesus like I've never seen Him before, and because of His grace, I can *IN-VISION* a brand new me.

In this story, we see Jesus unaffected by the wind and waves. As a matter of fact, He literally walked above the circumstances. That's where we should *IN-VISION* ourselves: above the circumstances, difficulties, and opposition.

Verse 30 says, *"But when Peter saw the wind, he was afraid and, beginning to sink, cried out, 'Lord, save me!'"*

Peter went from fearfully looking at the storm sinking his boat, to crying out to Jesus and walking above the circumstances by faith, only to go back to re-looking at and being moved by the circumstances. Don't let lifes obstacles cause you to vacillate and ruin your water-walk with Jesus.

Perhaps you're thinking, "I already did that, I've been there, I jumped out of the boat, I had an IN-VISION, I was focused, but I went back to looking at the situation and it's all over now."

The fact that you're reading this book proves it's not over! Look at something with me. In verse 30 of our story it says *"beginning to sink"* no one *begins* to sink; they just instantly sink. Step off of the edge of a pool onto the water and see if you *begin* to sink, like in slow motion. No, you don't *begin* to sink, you just sink.

What we see here is an amazing picture of the Grace of God. I want you to do the same: *IN-VISION* Jesus taking you by the hand, catching you, pulling you up, and telling you it's not over. See Him walking with you arm in arm to your desired destination.

The beauty of this story is that they experienced

the miracle of the five loaves and two fish on the one side of the lake, only to be told to go to the other side of the lake. Why? Why did Jesus say go to the other side of the lake? Because there was an even bigger miracle waiting on the other side.

Something Much Better Awaits You

Let's skip ahead to Matthew 14:34-36: *"When they had crossed over, they landed at Gennesaret. And when the men of that place recognized Jesus, they sent word to all the surrounding country. People brought all their sick to him and begged him to let the sick just touch the edge of his cloak, and all who touched him were healed." IN-VISION* that.

The miracle of feeding the multitude would fade quickly. It wouldn't be long until they were hungry again, but the physical healing that occurred on the other side of the lake would last a lifetime.

To *"IN-VISION"* is a practiced principle meant to last a lifetime, so don't get distracted, caught up in fear, feel like you're all alone and that you'll never make it. Revive the pictures of your life that you used to cherish, knowing that there's a huge blessing waiting for you on the other side of the lake despite the obstacle or circumstance you're currently facing.

So, when you hear the preaching of the Gospel, the Good News, the grace that has come from Jesus Christ, you must allow it to produce a picture in you of what God our Father really desires for your life. When you begin to see that Holy Spirit inspired mental photo, grab onto it, examine it, study it, sharpen it, memorize it, internalize it, and be determined to see its manifestation in your life!

Remember What the Word "IN-VISION" Means

To *IN-VISION* is to have a picture, a clear mental photograph of where you want your finances to be, the way you'd like your relationships to develop, what kind of job or career you desire, or what you'd like to do for your family, friends, church, and self. An *IN-VISION* is all about getting a picture on the inside of you, showing you what you want to be, where you want to go, what you want to do, or what you want to have.

This subject of *"IN-VISIONing"* is about changing the way you think and changing both the moving and still pictures you allow yourself to view over and over again in your mind. It's about meditating upon, pondering on, and staying focused on what you'd really like out of life. Webster's Dictionary says that the word, *"Envision,"* means, *"To send a picture to oneself."*

What kind of pictures have you been sending to yourself? Send yourself a mental photograph right now, showing you how much God loves you, and how wonderful a life He has prepared for you.

CHAPTER 5
Here's The Thing!

To *Envision* is "To Send a Picture to One's Self." *Envisioning* has to do with the mental pictures or images that you send to yourself. I like to say, *"IN-VISION,"* emphasizing the word, "IN," and meaning the vision or image or *PICTURE* you deliberately put "IN" your mind, hold "IN" your mind, and continually look at and refer to "IN" your mind. To put the right *PICTURE* or vision "IN" you – is to *"IN-VISION"* the right things.

Throughout your entire life, other people have been sending you *THEIR* pictures of you:

- What *THEY* thought of your potential.

- What *THEY* thought your faults and weaknesses looked like.

- What *THEY* thought that you could do and could not do.

- What *THEY* thought you do and do not deserve.

- What *THEY* picture you can and cannot accomplish.

- And how *THEY* think life works, including HOW your life must work.

Other people's conclusions about the government, economics, religion, morals, and happiness were *PHOTOGRAPHED* and *PHOTOSHOPPED* by *THEM*, and put into your *Mental Picture Album* for you to look at and memorize.

In addition to this, *PHOTOGRAPHS* containing attitudes about wealth and poverty, happiness and unhappiness, and how to think, react, and behave were also put into your *Mental Picture Album* by others, for you to look at, and memorize.

Generally speaking, the *PICTURES* they sent to you have now become the *PICTURES* you believe and live by. *THEIR PICTURES* have become your reality.

Here's the Thing

The pictures they sent you, were pictures that were

sent to them when they were young. In addition to this, the pictures they sent you were also based on their perceptions, attitudes, ignorance, misfortunes, beliefs, and experiences.

The Bible says, *"Every way (belief) of a man is right in his own eyes"* (Proverbs 21:2). It may be right in their own eyes, but it may not be right. It might be incapable of producing the results you desire. Although well-meaning, some of the pictures they sent you could be distorted, out of focus, or just plain harmful and wrong.

There's a popular computer program that takes your photographs of people and alters their faces by giving them funny bug eyes, big ears, or exaggerated features. We call this a "caricature." It resembles the person enough to identify who the photo is of, but something has been drastically changed.

Sometimes the pictures we have received from others or sent to ourselves are like caricatures. They resemble the truth but are distorted and not accurate.

On Facebook, it's my understanding that you can add a friend, delete a friend, or restrict a person's access to you. In the past, when we didn't know God, we gave Him no access to our lives, and we restricted Him from sending us the *PICTURES* He desired to put into our *Mental Picture Album* for us to look at, to memorize, and by which to be blessed.

Unfortunately, in addition to that, we allowed *TOTAL* access to people containing the wrong kind of information, to send us *THEIR PICTURES* to put into our *Mental Picture Album* for us to look at, to memorize, and by which to be harmed.

What You Have IN-VISIONed May be Hindering You

Job, in the Bible, *IN-VISIONed* (sent himself pictures of) his children disobeying God and bringing destruction upon themselves. Job acted in fear, based on the *PICTURES* he sent himself and viewed regularly, and, in doing so, brought calamity upon himself.

Elijah, the mighty prophet, after calling fire down out of heaven to consume the false prophets of Baal, IN-VISIONed Queen Jezebel having the power to kill him.

Mephibosheth, King Saul's Grandson, *IN-VISIONed* that King David hated him and wanted to kill him, when in reality, David wanted to bless him by restoring his full inheritance to him.

IN-VISION Success, Prosperity, Victory and Happiness

Start at once to send yourself different pictures.

Realize that the picture you have *"IN-VISIONed"* is what will reproduce itself on the outside, in your actual circumstances and life. Plaster so many *NEW PICTURES* on the bulletin board of your mind that you cover up the *"Can't do," "Will never have,"* and *"Don't deserve"* pictures that have filled your mind for so long.

Allow a different artist to paint on the canvas of your mind, covering up the old painting of insufficiency, ill-health, and failure. Let the new artist blot-out the old paintings with the crimson red paint of His blood and begin a new painting. IN-VISION a painting of unspeakable joy and a life of exciting purpose and fulfillment.

PICTURE yourself making friends with people easily. *PICTURE* yourself having doors of opportunity open for you, every day. *PICTURE* yourself having the skill level and confidence to take advantage of what God and life present to you. *PICTURE* yourself free from worry and stress and enjoying life.

Send Your Self a Picture of Victory

The enemy giant, Goliath, *IN-VISIONed* the young shepherd boy, David, being very easy to kill. David *IN-VISIONed* the opposite. He *IN-VISIONed* (sent himself a picture of) the huge body of Goliath lying dead on the ground. He *IN-VISIONed* the birds and wild animals eating his flesh. He *IN-VISIONed* Israel free from the menacing bully once and for all.

Jesus IN-VISIONed Both His and Your Victory

"Looking unto Jesus the author and finisher of our faith; who for the joy that was set before him endured the cross, despising the shame, and is set down at the right hand of the throne of God" (Hebrews 12:2).

I find it remarkable that Hebrews 12:2 says, *"For the joy that was set before him, he (Jesus) endured the cross."*

How is it possible to have joy set before you while at the same time enduring torture? Because Jesus *IN-VISIONed* the finished work of redemption.

Yes, the pain and suffering were very real and terrible; they had to be for Jesus to experience, as our substitute, what *WE* deserved. Yet, that's not what sustained Him hour after hour on the cross and occupied His thinking while on the cross. What sustained Him was He knew the pain would soon pass; He *IN-VISIONed* being raised from the dead and being crowned King of Kings and Lord of Lords.

Christ *IN-VISIONed* you redeemed and blessed, and *PICTURED* you in the family of God. What He *IN-VISIONed* while undergoing tremendous anguish and pain gave Him strength (the Bible even says, "Joy") to endure the torments of the cross.

Why not take a moment and ask Jesus to send you a *PICTURE* of how He IN-VISIONs you today. Remember, Hebrews 2:11 states that, *"Jesus is not ashamed to call us His brothers and sisters."* For that reason, He only has good pictures to send you. His *PICTURE* of you is of a champion, a winner, well supplied, moving in His wisdom and power, and having every reason to experience extreme happiness and courage. Why not make it a habit of looking at those pictures every day?

SEE the JOY

The tendency is to increase the number of *NEGATIVE PICTURES* you send yourself when you're experiencing a difficult time, but that's not what God wants you to do.

Jesus proved to us that when you're going through difficult times and struggling, a great key is to *SEE* the joy before you and *PICTURE* what you desire, not what is currently happening.

The time is going to pass anyway, so you might as well *IN-VISION* how you want your life to be in the future. In a real sense, you will be able to preview the wonderful life ahead of you, in advance, and prepare for it. What you *IN-VISION* becomes a blueprint or a road map for your life.

Remember, to *"IN-VISION"* is to send yourself a mental image or picture. It is what you visualize or see on the inside. *IN-VISION* (send yourself a picture of) you as the most noble, prosperous, happy, friendly, favored, and blessed person imaginable. Don't see yourself lacking anything. See every need, want, and desire fully met, in Jesus' Name!

Jesus IN-VISIONed Your Victory!
Now You Need to IN-VISION Your Victory, Too!

CHAPTER 6
SEE The Good!

Perhaps you are wondering why it's necessary to think about and *IN-VISION* what you desire, since happiness, success, victory, and prosperity, and the other great things you desire are the will of God for your life, anyway.

God's rich supply is all around you at all times and it is His will for you to experience it. However, the rich supply of God must be contacted, appropriated, and used.

Think of it this way: just because you live in an area that's close to a river or stream doesn't automatically mean that you are going to spontaneously be hydrated. You must still tap into and drink from the water that's available. What you think and believe, and particularly the images you hold in your mind, are your connection to God's rich supply.

It Works Both Ways!

Understand that the images you hold in your mind are a result of what you think and believe. Now, reverse it and it's still true. The images held in your mind will determine what you think and believe. Your attitudes, mental concepts, pictures, beliefs, and the way you view life are your connection with God's rich supply and your access to it; if your attitudes, mental concepts, pictures, and beliefs are negative, they become your connection with lack and want.

God can only do for you what He can do through you, by means of the beliefs, thoughts, and ideas leading to your actions. Prosperous *IN-VISIONing* opens a way to prosperous results.

If you want better financial conditions in your life, then don't picture or talk about financial lack, but began thinking, picturing, and talking in terms of rich abundance for your life. At all times keep in mind that God's supply is inexhaustible and He wants to lavishly and abundantly supply you with everything you need to grow, develop, and enjoy the life He has provided.

As you give up and cast away old ideas, attitudes, and beliefs that are incapable of producing desirable results, you must put in their place new ideas of prosperity, progress, and achievement. It won't be long before your conditions will steadily improve.

It should be obvious to you that the goal is not just to eliminate negative and harmful thoughts. That's a good thing to do, but if that's all you do, you will only create a vacuum that will suck in more negative stuff. The goal is to REPLACE the negative with the positive, especially replacing the negative with the promises of God's Word.

Like Joshua, as you meditate on, think about, and picture the promises of God being true in your situation, you get God involved in helping you. (See Joshua 1:8.) There must be constant elimination of the old unproductive ideas, thoughts, and pictures, in order to keep pace with growth and increase. By getting rid of the old discouraging and DISEMPOWERING thoughts, you make room for new powerful and productive thoughts.

Picture it like this: your respiratory system requires that you must first breathe out the oxygen depleted air from your lungs in order to take in new, oxygen rich, fresh air. When it comes to your respiratory system, if you do not breathe in new, fresh air, you will eventually suffocate.

In a real sense, many wonderful people's lives are being suffocated because they only think what they have always thought; they only picture what they've always pictured, nothing new.

I recently heard a story about a radio station contest. The idea was for people to drink several gallons of water and then to see how long they could wait before they urinated. The sad end to this story was that one lady actually died because of not releasing that which should have been eliminated. Her bladder burst and subsequently killed her.

Draw your own parallel here. If we're holding on to something that should've been released, what damage are we causing to our life and the lives of those we love?

The Law is clear here, just as our physical body needs to release the old *BEFORE* it can bring in the new, so it is with our *IN-VISIONing*. We must blow out the old unproductive *Mental Pictures* that hinder us from receiving new *Powerful* and *Productive Pictures* that we must have in order to obtain something new. The bottom line is that when you continue to look at the old picture albums of failure and lack, you hinder your advancement, or stop it altogether.

The First Step of Creating What You Desire

The first step to creating what you desire is to take your deep-seated longings, and, instead of suppressing them as *impossible dreams*, begin to visualize them, not just as a possibility, but as your reality. This principle goes along with what Jesus was saying in Mark 11:24 when He said, *"Believe you receive what you desire – when you pray!"*

It will be helpful to start doing something that is very simple but very much resisted in most people's lives. I myself resisted this principle for many years. Start by writing your desires down and then take the time to *VISUALIZE* what it is that you desire; *SEE* yourself in possession of what you desire.

The powerful principle of *IN-VISIONing* is simply sending yourself a mental picture of what you would like your conditions to be and then looking at your mental picture frequently, all the time improving the picture as you bring it more and more into focus. As you do that, you must hold fast to the firm belief that you will soon experience what your mental picture has shown you.

It's easy to gravitate to the thinking that if God would've wanted me to be happy and prosperous, He would have made me happy and prosperous. Realize that this is unreasonable and negative thinking. That's not how God or life works. God puts YOU in charge of your life and gives you the responsibility and authority to create your life the way you want it (Genesis 1:26-28, and Psalm 8).

Why is it Important for Me to Develop Mental Pictures?

Certainly, God could have created the world with every imaginable thing already created and made. But He takes delight in allowing and empowering people to create the things that make for a better life, and makes them happy as individuals.

If you are currently experiencing financial troubles, you will continue to have financial problems until you change your mental images. While you are thinking about, talking about, and picturing financial lack, your mind is producing what you are imaging. Change your images and think, talk, and *PICTURE PLENTY*, and you shall have it!

God says, *"Poverty and shame shall be to him that refuses instruction"* (Proverbs 13:18). Did you notice that God equates poverty and shame together? I taught a series at our church called, *"Shame OFF You."* We could say in context of Proverbs 13:18, that since God wants *Shame OFF You*, He must also want *Poverty OFF You*, since this verse says that they go together.

Because God wants both shame and poverty off of your life, you should immediately stop *PICTURING* yourself in a shameful and poverty-stricken condition. So that you don't create a vacuum, you should immediately replace those negative thoughts by *PICTURING* yourself as honorable and prosperous.

CHAPTER 7
IN-VISION Your Success

The imaging power of the mind, which some consider to have an almost magical creative power, should be invoked to work for you every day. In his classic book, _Think and Grow Rich_, Napoleon Hill said, _"What the mind can conceive and believe, it can achieve."_

A study on the mind might show that man can create anything he can imagine. Everything from a simple paperclip to a complex Space Station started as an image in someone's mind.

Modern science has confirmed that the _Mental Image_ (IN-VISION) held in a person's mind does, in actuality, create the conditions and experiences of that person's life and affairs. Even Albert Einstein agreed that man's only limitations lie in the negative use of his imagination. Stated another way, "What limits us is our *IN-VISIONing* of the wrong things."

Understand what Albert Einstein was saying. If there is failure and lack in your life, it is because you first imagined it in your mind. What you actually did was send yourself a *Mental Picture* of failure and lack; you then looked at that picture long enough to actually produce failure and lack in your experience.

You first set up your limitations in your mind before you ever experienced limitations in your life!

You bought into the limiting pictures you sent yourself and soon you experienced what those pictures portrayed. Now is the time to start sending yourself and start using the correct *Mental Pictures* to begin dissolving those self-made limitations, remaking your life in a way that will delight you.

Imagination is Stronger than Willpower

Doctor, Emile Coue', (1857-1926), was a brilliant French psychologist and pharmacist who introduced popular principles of psychotherapy and self-improvement based on positive self-talk or what he called, "optimistic auto-suggestion." He is credited with discovering what we know today as the *"placebo effect."*

Dr. Coue' and his wife founded *The Lorraine Society of Applied Psychology* in France in 1913; his popular book… <u>*Self-Mastery Through Conscious Autosuggestion*</u> was embraced and extensively taught by such men as Dr. Norman Vincent Peale, Robert H. Schuller, and W. Clement Stone.

Perhaps you've heard a pastor or success motivation speaker encourage people to regularly say, "Day by day, in every way, I'm getting better and better." That mantra came from Emile Coue'.

Unlike a commonly held belief that a strong *WILL* constitutes the best path to success, Coue' maintained that curing some of our troubles requires a change in our unconscious thought, which can be achieved only by using our *IMAGINATION*. Although stressing that he was not primarily a healer, but one who taught others how to heal themselves, Coue' claimed to have effected organic changes through autosuggestion.

Coue' described autosuggestion as… "An instrument we possess at birth, with which we play unconsciously all our life, as a baby plays with its rattle. It is, however, a dangerous instrument; it can wound, or even kill you, if you handle it imprudently and unconsciously. It can, on the contrary, save your life when you know how to employ it consciously."

Because we are talking about *IN-VISIONing*, let me paraphrase how Coue' described autosuggestion using the word *IN-VISION*.

"*IN-VISION* is an instrument that we possess at birth, which we unconsciously use all of our life. The power to *IN-VISION* is, however, a dangerous instrument; it can wound or even kill you if you handle it imprudently and unconsciously. On the contrary, it can enhance, bless, and even save your life when you know how to employ it consciously and correctly."

Doctor Emile Coue' was among the first to discover that the imagination is a much stronger force than willpower, that when the imagination and the will are in conflict, the imagination always wins out.

For example, a child imagining a scary monster under his bed in the middle of the night may *WILL* himself not to be afraid. Yet, inevitably, his imagination wins out and he seeks the safety that can only be found by sticking his head under the covers. This demonstrates how imagination is stronger than willpower.

Often, when a mental picture of some desirable blessing, such as prosperity, success, happiness, joy, and favor is first suggested, your logic and will does not want to accept such a foreign and outrageous picture. The mental picture of those wonderful things may seem too fantastic and too amazing to be true and real for you.

Sarah had a hard time believing that she could have a baby because of her and Abraham's old age. At first, she laughed at what God promised because her *LOGIC* rejected the mental picture of her having a baby (Genesis 18:12).

Think... View... Focus... Repeat...!

When a mental picture is repeatedly viewed and focused on, the imagination has no choice but to accept it and aid in bringing it to pass, no matter how unlikely the mental picture first appears to the reasoning power of your mind.

That's really good news, because as you *IN-VISION* what you desire, there will eventually be a turnaround in what you think is possible for you.

Your logic and will may fight you at first, but *CONTINUE* sending yourself Pictures of what you want to become and what you want to have and do.

As we study and apply the Law of *IN-VISIONing* Success and Prosperity, determined to only *IN-VISION* prosperity and success, we are not trying to hypnotize ourselves into thinking or doing something outlandish. Instead, we are *de-hypnotizing* ourselves from the negative programs and the ignorant, superstitious, and limiting beliefs of centuries of poverty thoughts.

Since you are believing God for greater happiness and good in your life, you should immediately begin to form the *Mental Image* of the happiness and good you wish to experience. Do this until you get the *PICTURE PERFECT*, at which time you will be experiencing the happiness and good you desire and you deserve.

Your reasoning power may tell you that what you desire can never happen, but that doesn't matter. What you desire will happen if you will destroy the old, limiting, can't have, can't do, *Picture Album* that you've been looking at every day and start creating a new *Picture Album* filled with the wonderful photos of what you want to become and experience.

Imagination is Greater than Reasoning

It seemed unreasonable to think that man would ever be able to fly through the air. It seemed unreasonable to think that man could speak into a device without wires and talk to someone on the other side of the world. When you think about it, almost everything we take for granted and experience daily was, at one time, *imaginable*, but seemed *unreasonable*, maybe even impossible.

Your logic and will may insist that your dream is too big to come true and that it is impossible to fulfill. But if you will just disregard the largeness of your dream and dare to continue *IN-VISIONing* and imagining it anyway, your imagination, along with your subconscious mind, in cooperation with the creative power of God within you, will go to work for you to produce the visible results you have been desiring and imagining.

Whatever the mind is taught to expect, it will build, produce, and bring it forth for you (good or bad).

Imagine with Purpose!

The *Peloponnesian War* of ancient Greece lasted twenty-seven years because both sides lacked purpose and strategy. They had no real plan of action, no gumption, and no real passion for victory.

The war became an acceptable, mundane way of life. Don't you dare allow your life to slip by the way the Grecian's did. The mediocre and mundane existence that you've experienced in the past has no place in your future.

Often, we resemble those Greeks in that we have no plan or image of victory; we just continue along with a mediocre life, never quite winning and never quite losing, just continually struggling and fighting without gaining headway.

When you use the imaging power of your mind to *IN-VISION* your good, you are using the most direct method that will secure for you the victory over life's problems. Instead of battling with poverty, failure, and financial lack, which often only multiplies your problems, begin using God's ordained method – that of quietly, deliberately, and persistently *IMAGING* yourself with the blessings He promised and you desire.

Vision is Victory

Joseph dreamed about and *IN-VISIONed* himself with authority and dominion and so must you. Joseph dreamed of dominion, wealth, and influence when it seemed like he had none and so must you. Success is always created mentally, first.

In Joseph's case, he made the mistake of telling his dreams and *IN-VISION* to his jealous brothers, who resented his claims of success and dominion; they betrayed him and sold him for twenty pieces of silver to some Ishmaelite merchants on their way to Egypt.

Unlike Joseph, you should be very guarded about telling your dreams and mental images of greater success and good to others. More times than not, they will only try to blur your *Picture* of grandeur with their fear, doubt, criticism, and negativity.

Since the old saying is true, "Misery loves company," if your family and friends can't *SEE* success, happiness, and prosperity for themselves, they sure don't want to *SEE* it for you.

After Joseph was sold into Egypt and slavery, he obviously continued to visualize a much better life than what he was presently experiencing. He proved that vision is victory; he also proved that by keeping the correct *Picture* in mind and viewing it regularly, the victim will become the victor!

Persist in Picturing Success

Continually imagine the standard of living you want for yourself and your family. Do you want to own your own spacious, comfortable home? Do you want to own several dependable cars? Do you want to travel and vacation to wonderful places around the world?

Do you want to give in a bigger way to help your church and help the needy? Then persist in picturing those things, especially when circumstances scream, *"It will never happen, never happen, never happen!"*

For some people, it may actually take them a year or more to convince their own mind that these great things are possible and available for them. Since the time is going to pass anyway, why not utilize that time to make a better future for yourself and for those you love?

For most people, it takes the mind a while to accept rich *Mental Pictures*, because thoughts of success, prosperity, and happiness are so foreign and contrary to how they have thought in the past. Again, since the time is going to pass anyway, you have nothing to lose and everything to gain by only thinking in rich mental pictures.

After your mind becomes fully convinced that God wants you to prosper, has made wonderful provision for you to prosper, and that you can become prosperous, it's like breaking a hard shell: suddenly, success will begin to come so fast that it will be hard to keep up with.

Regardless of how long it takes, keep sending yourself *Pictures* of success, viewing those pictures daily, and adding details to them; keep holding fast to the high standard of living that you desire and that God has provided for you through the redemptive work of Jesus Christ.

Charles Fillmore once described the terrific power of imagination when he wrote, *"Imagination gives man the ability to project himself through time and space and rise above all limitations."*

Napoleon Used the Law of IN-VISIONing

"So we fix our eyes not on what is seen, but on what is unseen. For what is seen is temporary, but what is unseen is eternal" (2 Cor 4:18 NIV).

To *"fix our eyes"* means to stay focused upon what it is you're considering and desiring. When our eyes are not *FIXED*, we're gazing and meditating upon things that we really don't desire. Please notice that your eyes need to be focused upon something that, according to this verse, can't be recognized by your five physical senses. This verse says it's *"unseen."*

Just as perfume is non-existent to the sense of hearing, so what you're *IN-VISIONing* does not *YET* exist in your now experience.

Napoleon kept a huge map before him with colored

flags indicating the various moves he planned, months in advance, for his army to take. He wrote down his desires and plans, so as to clarify them and put them into action in the invisible realm before he even started to deal with them in the physical realm.

IN-VISIONing (which is sending yourself *Mental Pictures*) starts the creative process of what you desire in the invisible realm. That means that aid and assistance can go before you, into your future, and start working on your behalf before *YOU* ever arrive in your future.

By using mental pictures, Napoleon became victorious in the invisible realm before his soldiers ever drew a sword in the physical realm. Historians say that he dictated in detail the order and length of the marches, the meeting places of the two armies, how he would attack, the movement of the enemy, how they would attack, and even the blunders he expected the enemy to make, several months before it happened, and at a distance of seven hundred miles away from the scene of battle.

Napoleon used his imagination and the power of *IN-VISIONing* to conquer much of the known world. You can use the same formula to conquer your world!

The Picture You SEE Determines
The Difference Between Success and Failure

Imagination can turn your current thought and expectation from *"I can't have"* to *"I can and will have,"* from despair to hope, from failure to success, from discouragement to encouragement, from insufficiency to abundance.

Like many before me, I am discovering that the *Law of IN-VISIONing Success and Prosperity* is fascinating and extremely rewarding!

As impossible as it may seem today, the more you develop it, the more it will seem that the world around you rushes towards you in a friendly fashion, only too happy to grant your desires. I have also discovered and can tell you assuredly that most people will continue having financial problems until they first change their mental images.

If you are thinking about, talking about, and *Picturing* financial lack, all you will be able to produce in your life is the physical equivalence of what you are imaging: lack! Change your images. Think, talk, and *Picture* abundance, and you shall have abundance.

Usually, what we see depends mainly on what we look for. Often life's results are the difference between the constructive or destructive mental images that you entertain for yourself and about others.

Your imagination loves to be given definite pictures to build blueprints; your subconscious mind then gratefully accepts and gets busy producing the blueprints as definite results for you.

Actually, you have been using the power of *Visualization* and *Imagination* all your life. However, you probably haven't been using it to *deliberately* receive what you desire from God and life. Perhaps you have visualized and imagined insufficient faith, lack of money, lack of success, poor health, bad relationships, working for years on a job that you hate, and many other things you don't really want in your life.

A great key to success is to stop *Imagining* and *Picturing* the things you don't want (the opposite of what you do want) and start *Imagining* and *Picturing* ONLY the things you do want.

Take your wallet or purse in your hand during your quiet time. Close your eyes and mentally imagine bills of large denomination bulging from the wallet or purse. *Mentally Picture* your deposit slips showing large amounts of money being deposited in your bank accounts. Imagine all the good things you wish to experience and every day add more and more delightful details.

Mentally imagine the way you wish to conduct your life. *Picture* yourself with the favor, poise, graciousness, confidence, respect, talent, and professionalism that you wish to display.

The More You Deliberately and Purposefully Use the Imaging Power of Your Mind, the More Powerfully it Will Work for You!

You are constantly sending yourself *mental pictures*, whether you have been aware of it or not. Why not send yourself *pictures* of the "you" that you want to be, possessing the things you desire to have? By taking conscious control of your imagining power, you can produce and start experiencing the health, wealth, and happiness that is yours by divine right.

Don't compromise in the area of your *Mental Picture Taking*. Imagine what you really want, not just what you think you can possibly have if you are lucky. Pay no attention to your will and reason, which will try to talk you out of your mental images. Your active imagination will soon take control of your will and put it in its place if you will first take control of your imagination by feeding it the *Mental Pictures* of what God promised you, those that you deeply and sincerely want.

If you feed your imagination half-hearted, lukewarm, and contradicting mental pictures, you will get those kinds of results. God said that a double minded man, a person of two opinions, shouldn't even *THINK* he will receive anything from the Lord (James 1:6-8).

You wouldn't want to look at a photo album full of out of focus, blurry pictures, would you? In the same way, the creative part of your being doesn't want to view vague and foggy pictures. Focus.

The Image Produces the Condition

Truly, the image produces the condition. If you will make the mental image of what you desire vivid and hold on to that image, the condition that matches that image will materialize.

The reason that God commanded you to *CAST DOWN* negative thoughts, unscriptural reasoning, and harmful *MENTAL PICTURES* in 2 Corinthians 10:5 is to strip those negative things of their power to produce something detrimental in your life.

In the above reference, God is clearly telling us that negative thoughts and *MENTAL PICTURES*, if uninterrupted, will materialize.

Create a Dream or Vision Board

If you do not presently have confidence that your desire can come true, it will certainly help to place a physical picture or photograph of what you desire where you can view it daily. This process is called, *"Creating a Dream Board or Vision Board."*

To physically see an image of what you desire helps to imprint on your mind the image of what you desire. When you can see it in your mind – you can have it in time. Your subconscious mind will embrace the image on your Vision Board and your desires will come to pass.

This principle also works in other areas. If, for example, you would like to own a beautiful home that is currently beyond your financial means, it will be beneficial for you to make a regular practice of walking through and checking out Model Homes. In fact, you can make this process enjoyable and fun.

If a beautiful home is what you desire, why not make the commitment to go out to lunch with your family and then take them to visit Model Homes every Sunday, after church, for the next couple of months? It can be a family adventure.

As you and your family see the openness, elegance,

and craftsmanship of expensive Model Homes, something inside of you and your family will eventually say, "Yeah, I can own a house like this." At that point it will be much easier for you to *IN-VISION* yourself owning and enjoying that home, or a similar home, because you have seen it with your physical eyes.

Things are easier to see in your *mind's* eye if you have already seen something similar with your physical eyes. Your imagination makes the equivalent physical condition, but it's up to you to clarify and develop the image of the condition you want to receive.

Get busy, or maybe I should say, "Slow down," and quietly imagine, in detail, all that you wish to be, do, and have. Soon, what was once a deliberately forced mental condition will become your reality.

It is true that a man becomes what he imagines. It is also true that continuous proper imagination is sufficient to create or re-create your life for the better. By filling your mind with the mental images that would delight you, your mind is then given the confidence and nourishment to turn those mental images into visible results.

The Mind Delights to Create and Experience What it Imagines!

CHAPTER 8
What's Your Issue?

The principle I've been sharing with you of *IN-VISIONing*, although not mentioned as such prominently, lies under the surface of nearly every Bible story that God has recorded for our benefit.

IN-VISION Victory When Facing Insurmountable Odds

God certainly required Joshua to *IN-VISION* the military fortress of Jericho, with its impenetrable walls, crumbling before the children of Israel. The Lord said to Joshua, *"SEE (send this PICTURE to yourself), I have given into your hand Jericho, and the king thereof, and the mighty men of valor"* (Joshua 6:2).

For the word *"SEE,"* the Message Bible uses, "Look sharp now." What this means to me is that God was telling Joshua to get a sharp, focused, high definition *Mental Picture*, or a *Picture Perfect* Image, of the walls falling down. A few days later, they did. What Joshua *PICTURED*, happened.

Anything They Envisioned was Possible for Them

The rebellious people who followed Nimrod *IN-VISIONed* building a city with a tower that would reach up into the heavens. Rather than scatter abroad and replenish the earth, as God had commanded, they decided to stay together, sin together, and build a waterproof tower higher than the clouds so that even a flood, similar to the flood of Noah, which had previously wiped wickedness off the earth, could not wipe them out. They then purposed to establish worship to the constellations and zodiac, in rebellion to God's command.

Although the Bible uses the word *"imagined,"* we could easily substitute the word, *"IN-VISIONed."* The creative power of Unity and *IN-VISIONing* was so great that God had to come down and confound their language in order to break the limitless power of their agreement and the potential of their accomplishments.

"And the Lord said, 'Behold, they are one people and they have all one language; and this is only the beginning of what they will do, and now nothing they have imagined (IN-VISIONed) they can do will be impossible for them" (Genesis 11:6, Amplified Bible).

Moses' Victory was Based on What He IN-VISIONed

The Bible is very clear about how Moses endured hardships and overcame obstacles:

"Anticipating the payoff, Moses had his eye on (IN-VISIONed) the One no one can see, and kept right on going" (Hebrews 11:26-27, Message Bible).

"It was faith that made Moses leave Egypt without being afraid of the king's anger as though he saw (IN-VISIONed) the invisible God" (Hebrews 11:27 Good News Bible).

Moses was a winner because he continually *IN-VISIONed* that God was with him, God was for him, and God was his protector and provider. You need to *IN-VISION* the same things.

How This Applied to Others

In John, chapter 11, at the tomb of Lazarus, Jesus *IN-VISIONed* Lazarus being raised from the dead. When He tried to get Martha to *IN-VISION* the same thing, she couldn't.

The four men carrying their buddy on a stretcher, taking him to where Jesus was, *IN-VISIONed* that if they somehow got their friend in the presence of Jesus, Jesus would heal him (Luke 5:18-25). And Jesus did.

Although he could not see, blind Bartimaeus *IN-VISIONed* (sent himself a mental picture) that if he could just get in the presence of his Messiah, Jesus, his vision would be restored (Mark 10:46). And it was.

After the remarkable miracle that the woman with the issue of blood experienced, a multitude of people *IN-VISIONed* that if they touched the hem of Jesus' garment, they also would be healed. *"And as many as touched him were made perfectly whole"* (Luke 6:19).

In the book of Acts, a great number of people *IN-VISIONed* that if they simply had the shadow of Peter pass over them, they would be healed (Acts 5:15). And they were.

The Bible tells us that we are to not look at the things that are seen, because the things that are seen are temporary (subject to change) but we are to look at the things that are not seen (the things God has promised us and the things we desire) because those things are eternal (2 Corinthians 4:18).

Abraham was given all the land that he could *SEE* (Genesis 13:15).

David *IN-VISIONed* that Goliath would be as easy to kill as a lion or a bear and *visualized* him dead (1 Samuel 17:37-58) and he was.

Three Hebrew boys *IN-VISIONed* that the God that they served continually was able to deliver them out of the burning fiery furnace (Daniel 3:17) and He did.

A whole city *IN-VISIONed* that if they waited at the door where Jesus was staying, He would come out and heal them (Mark 1:33-34) and He did.

Peter affirmed that he *IN-VISIONed* that Jesus is the Christ, the Son of the living God (Matthew 16:16).

On and on we could go throughout the Bible about how *IN-VISIONing* was an underlying factor in people's victory (or demise in some cases).

How could God possibly declare the end from the beginning, and call those things that be not as though they were, if He couldn't *IN-VISION* what He was speaking? See Isaiah 46:10 and Romans 4:17.

I want to share with you the events that I *IN-VISION* transpired in the life of the woman that was bleeding to death, talked about in Mark 5, a viewpoint a little different than the one usually taken.

The Woman With the Issue of Blood

The basket in her hand seemed heavier today as she walked among the vendors searching for just the right grapes, dates, avocados, and pomegranates. She purchased the fish and bread she would need today, yesterday.

She usually carried herself with an air of confidence and nobility that made her even more attractive than her beautiful looks. She was well respected in the community and among the merchants.

She had many friends in the open market. This morning, she was mainly looking for some fruit; she would then return home to make lunch for herself and a friend from out of town that would be visiting her around noon.

Her husband had died thirteen months earlier and a number of close friends had been faithfully keeping her company, several days a week. Today though, for some reason, she didn't feel the zest for life that she had always known, as long as she could remember.

Recognizing that something was wrong, her friend suggested at lunch that she go see her cousin, a local physician, and maybe with the correct medicine or herbs she could regain her enthusiasm and vigor.

So she made the appointment and met with her friend's cousin who immediately put her on a special diet that had helped several of his patients; he also gave her a jar of nasty tasting powder to mix with water and drink twice a day. Yet, within the next two months her health continued to deteriorate, even more rapidly. The medicine and diet didn't seem to be helping.

When she went to the market in the morning, the vendors noticed that the spring in her step was gone. She was starting to look haggard and sickly. Her doctor noticed her alarming decline and recommended a colleague in Decapolis, who treated her, but produced no encouraging results.

So began a twelve-year quest to be healed. Without a husband to take her to distant lands seeking the newest cures, travel would be quite difficult and expensive, but if she could get her health back, it would all be worth it.

She traveled far and wide seeking help, including two trips to Arabia. Her journey ended with a four-month stay in Nain, where the greatest doctors of her day treated the most difficult cases. It was there that she ran out of money and decided to return home to die where she had been brought up.

Her body, which was once so alive and strong, vibrant and beautiful, now seemed like it was her enemy. Every day she felt more frail and weak than the day before. Her beautiful flowing thick hair had thinned out considerably, gray now replacing her beautiful black head of hair, and the sun-like glow of her complexion now looked pale.

She Was Sent a Picture of Death

After spending all the money she had, she had been diagnosed with an incurable issue of blood. Her constant bleeding was causing her life to flow out of her slowly, but at a steady rate, and no one was able to stop the flow.

Under the Law of Moses, her condition meant that she was declared "unclean" and could no longer interact with society, including her friends, family, and her many acquaintances at the marketplace.

While he was alive, her husband and she had made many quality friendships in the community. Although many of her friends felt it was best to stay away from her, some still came to visit, bringing her fruit and vegetables, fish and grain, from the market place.

She looked forward to the wonderful visits from her friends so that they could catch her up on the news that was happening in town and the people she loved. One day, one of her friends told her about something amazing she had observed the previous week.

A Friend Sent Her a Picture of Hope

She said she was in a neighboring town about twenty miles away visiting her sister when she saw a man named Jesus teaching in the town square and healing all who were sick and infirmed. Her friend began to tell her about all the wonderful things Jesus had to say and all the wonderful help He provided for that community by telling them about God's goodness and by healing the sick folks.

As her friend spoke, hope began to spring-up in this noble, but frail woman. From that day forward, she began to ask everyone that visited her if they had any news about the man named Jesus. Most didn't, but some did. The fame of Jesus was growing. And as she heard the stories of the compassion of Jesus and His willingness to heal the most difficult cases, she began to say, both out loud and within herself, *"If I can just touch His garment, I know I will be healed."*

Although she slept much of the day, in her waking moments, as she would do whatever necessary tasks she could that day, she kept saying out loud, *"If I but touch hem of His garment, I will be healed"* (Mark 5:28).

Without even knowing it, by sharing what she knew about the love of Jesus and His power to heal, her friend had planted a Picture inside the mind of the dying noble woman. She *IN-VISIONed* what Jesus must have looked like. She *IN-VISIONed* Him speaking with authority to crowds, teaching them about the things of God, miraculously feeding the hungry multitudes, and then healing all that were sick.

Even more importantly, she now *IN-VISIONed* herself somehow getting to Jesus, touching His clothes, and receiving what all of her money and all of her doctors couldn't give her — healing and life.

In her pain and suffering she lost track of how much time had gone by since she had first heard of Jesus. But every day she was faithful to say aloud over and over, "When I touch the clothes of Jesus, I will be made whole." And every day she was diligent to view and add details to what she had been *visualizing*.

Within a few months, the day came that Jesus and His disciples were headed for her town. Her friends rushed to her home to tell her that Jesus was coming the next morning.

She awoke early the following morning and struggled to get dressed. She forced herself out of her house and into the sunlit outdoors, which seemed harsh and blinding to her. She willed her legs to step forward and walk into the daylight towards the center of town.

Soon she saw a huge multitude gathering near the marketplace. People were pushing, shoving, and pressing to get to Jesus. It seemed like a dangerous situation for someone in her condition to have to contend with.

Was it just too much to push herself to get to where Jesus was? She knew she would have to probably crawl under people's legs, maybe shove people aside, and possibly even be rude in order to get where Jesus was.

Over the weeks since she first heard of Jesus she had been sending herself Pictures of this moment. It had played out in her imagination many times. She was at the Red Sea of her life. Either God would come through for her and she would be healed or He wouldn't and she would be dead in a month or two.

It's Now or Never

She knew in her heart she would probably be too weak; she would even possibly die before she had another opportunity to act out what she had been *visualizing* and *affirming* concerning her healing. Although it was inconvenient and difficult, now was her time.

Through sheer determination to realize what she had been continually saying and *IN-VISIONing*, she forged forward, closer to Jesus. There, after having been knocked down by the crowd and on her hands and knees, she stretched out her hand and barely touched the border of His robe.

Like a bolt of lightning, power flashed from Jesus' body into hers and she was instantly and miraculously healed of her plague.

As I mentally tried to put *flesh-and-blood* on the woman's backstory, that's the way I *IN-VISIONed* it from Mark 5. I wrote that she was healed *"instantly."* But as you can clearly see, her healing was a process. It took the noble woman a certain amount of time to declare what she wanted, by faith, and get a clear Mental Picture of her healing before the day came that she was *instantly* healed.

Her words and the Pictures she sent to herself continually, set the stage for her *"Instantly."* What she had *IN-VISIONed* was now her reality, just as yours will be if you say and send yourself Pictures of what you desire from God and life.

Her story proves to us that the word, *"Incurable"* (IN-Curable), can really mean, *"Only Curable from Within."* After spending all of her money on many doctors, she was not better, she only grew worse. She was only curable from within.

Perhaps, like the woman in our story, you have tried many things to solve or resolve what's troubling you. Your trouble might be physical, financial, or relational, but I have found that many of the difficulties we encounter in life are incurable: *Only Curable from Within*, as you think and *IN-VISION* properly.

CHAPTER 9
Close Your Eyes and Visualize!

Perhaps you've heard of the co-author of _Chicken Soup for the Soul_, Jack Canfield. The _Chicken Soup for the Soul_ book series currently has more than two hundred titles and five hundred copies sold worldwide. It's a huge success.

Jack Canfield said that he grew up in extreme poverty. He said that his dad was very negative, thinking that rich people were only rich because they ripped somebody off or deceived someone. He grew up hearing negative slogans from his dad such as, _"Money doesn't grow on trees," "Put it back; we can't afford it,"_ and _"Who do you think I am, a Rockefeller?"_

Jack grew up being programmed with a lot of wrong beliefs and _Mental Pictures_ about money. He believed that if you had it, it made you bad, and he truly believed that life was supposed to be hard and difficult, a struggle.

Later in life, though, he started to work with businessman, philanthropist, and self-help book author, W. Clement Stone, who challenged him to set a financial goal so big for himself that if he achieved it, it would blow his mind. He was told that if he achieved it, he would know that it was because he put into practice the principles that Clement Stone had taught him.

(It may be of interest to you to know that W. Clement Stone (1902-2002) gave over two hundred and seventy-five million dollars to charity, including civic groups, mental health causes, and Christian organizations; he created his great wealth beginning with only one hundred dollars and some of the principles that I'm teaching you in this book.)

At the time of Clement Stone's challenge, Jack Canfield was making about eight thousand dollars a year. He said that he wanted to set a goal that was really measurable, so he set his goal to make one hundred thousand dollars a year. I guess he thought that going from eight thousand dollars a year to one hundred thousand dollars a year would be measurable.

At the time, he felt like he had no strategy, no possibility of making that much money, and no ideas on how it could be done, but he said, "I'm going to declare it, believe it, act as if it were true, and release it."

One of the things that Clement Stone taught him about success and creating wealth was to close his eyes every day for a few minutes and *VISUALIZE* the goal as if it were already achieved. Hey, that sounds like the principle of sending yourself a *PICTURE!*

Jack Canfield took a one-dollar bill and a Sharpie marker and wrote *"$100,000"* on the one-dollar bill. He put it on the ceiling of his bedroom so that when he woke up in the morning, he would *SEE* a one-hundred-thousand-dollar bill and it would remind him that one hundred thousand dollars a year was his intention.

After he was reminded of his intention, he then closed his eyes and *VISUALIZED* having a one-hundred-thousand-dollar-a-year lifestyle.

The first year of *VISUALIZING* his goal, he said that a little over ninety thousand dollars came in. He didn't reach his one-hundred-thousand-dollar goal, but claims he wasn't discouraged about going from eight thousand dollars a year to over ninety thousand dollars a year. Jack was obviously persuaded that what W. Clement Stone taught about *visualizing* your desire and your goals was true. It really works!

The Next Step Was a One Million Dollar Goal

Jack Canfield's next goal was to create one million dollars by thinking positive and *VISUALIZING* one million dollars. Obviously, he created and experienced his dream, but it wasn't by random luck or by working his fingers to the bone. Although he didn't say it exactly the way I'm saying it in this book, his success was accomplished by faithfully sending himself and regularly viewing the right kind of *MENTAL PICTURES*.

As Jack was faithful to *VISUALIZE* his goals, something amazing happened in the process. Ideas began to float into his consciousness, that when acted upon, created opportunities and prosperity.

The same thing will happen to you when you are diligent to use this God-given key to success. The Holy Spirit will begin to impart to you, ideas, that when acted upon, will also bring you greater opportunities and more prosperity.

For many of us, the first time we hear this principle of *VISUALIZING* or sending ourselves *PICTURES* of what we desire, it may seem like a waste of time. But it's not!

W. Clement Stone created a company worth over one billion dollars, many years ago, which enabled him to give millions of dollars to charity. More recently, Jack Canfield, helped create the _Chicken Soup for the Soul_ book series, which has encouraged and blessed the lives of millions of people and created amazing wealth for him and his family.

You must understand that before God spoke into existence the things He created in Genesis 1, He had to have _VISUALIZED_ what He wanted before He could speak what He wanted. God _VISUALIZED_ what He wanted and then _SPOKE_ what He wanted. And it happened. I'm simply encouraging you to do it God's way, and imitate God.

For that reason, don't even entertain the idea that _IN-VISIONing_ is a waste of time. If you stick with it, _IN-VISIONing_ will change your life!

What Do You Want From God and Life?

Along with sending yourself a mental picture, _IN-VISIONing_ means mentally _SEEING_ yourself the way you desire be, having the things you desire to have, and doing the things you desire to do.

Jack Canfield desired and intended to help people, and became a millionaire in the process. What do you desire and intend to become, have, and do?

The Word "SEE" is in the Word Seed

When you *MENTALY SEE* the things you desire and see those things very clearly, you are in harmony with God and His method of creating. Then, like what happens when a seed is planted into the creative soil of the ground, God's Spirit begins to transform and grow your intentions into their usable, tangible, and manifested form. In other words, you soon have what you *IN-VISIONed*.

It's interesting that the word *"SEE"* is in the word, *"SEED."* What you *SEE* is a *SEED* to your future. Both are capable of producing after their own kind. Good or bad.

If the thought image you are creating and pondering is distinct, focused, and clear, it provides a good pattern for God to work with. If the thought image is blurred, distorted, incomplete, or imperfect, the pattern of what you desire is less than adequate and cannot be replicated positively into your experience; thus, the need to think and *IN-VISION* clearly about what it is you really want.

Your PICTURE Connects You to the Creative Factory of God

The first thing to do is to decide what is within you and all around you that you wish to turn over to the Creative Factory of God. What do you wish to have manufactured? You start by deciding what you want and then continue by sending yourself *PICTURES* of what you wish to have manufactured and experienced in your life.

After having become *COMPOSED* in thought, begin to *SEE* the completed outcome of your desires in *MENTAL PICTURES*. This enables the creative process and the laws that God has established to begin to work on your desired project.

Suppose that you desire to obtain a home. You should know just what kind of home you desire. Of course, if you simply thought of an unspecific, common house, you would certainly get something, but the clearer the *PICTURE* you send to yourself, the better your results will be and the more certain your success will be.

In order to make your picture or *IN-VISION* complete, decide just what kind of a home you wish to live in. Then, in the silence of your thought, mentally look at your house.

Through practice, you will soon be able to get to the place, in your mind, where you can go from room to room and be sure it is laid-out exactly the way you want it. Mentally stop here and there to look at some piece of furniture or at some picture on the wall. In your mind, enter your house, sit down and feel that you are actually living there. As you view your mental images of the house say, "I am now living in my dream house."

Make the whole thing real, as far as possible, in the *MENTAL PICTURE* you are observing.

It will take focus, concentration, and practice to get to the place where your sanctified imagination gets used to forming these mental pictures so accurately. Not to worry, your expertise at *IN-VISIONing* will grow with practice. By doing this, you have set a creative image in motion which will bring a realization of your desire, unless you, yourself, neutralize the picture by blurring it with doubt. Continue doing this exercise every day until the house you have been *IN-VISIONing,* appears.

Use this same process in visualizing *"What things so ever you desire"* (Mark 11:24). Another way to say this verse is, *"What things so ever you IN-VISION when you pray, believe you will receive what you IN-VISIONed and you will have it."*

In order that you may fully understand just what I mean and how this works, I will illustrate by drawing a mental picture which I will ask you to follow and *IN-VISION* as you read these lines.

Imagine that you and I are together. We will suppose that I am a large man about six feet and three inches tall with short dark hair and a goatee. We are sitting on the front porch of a rural house, drinking iced tea. Can you see it? It's a white two-story house and it sits quite far back from the road. A few hundred feet away there are tall trees and the sun is shining through the trees in front of the house.

We can see a mixture of sunlight and shadows upon the porch through the open spaces between the branches of the trees. The breeze is gently blowing and the leaves are waving back and forth, letting in the sunlight. I say to you, "Let's take a walk together." We immediately rise from our seats, which are made of wicker, and walk down three wooden steps to a gravel walkway, leading to the road.

As we go out through a wooden gate leading to the road, a dog that is jogging along the road suddenly meets us. He is a large, brown dog and is jogging, but not quite running. We watch him as he jogs past us, down the road, until he rounds a bend in the road and is gone.

Now, did you imagine that story by thinking about mere words, or did you *SEE PICTURES* in your mind as the story unfolded? If you carefully imagined each picture as it occurred in the above story, you understand what visualizing means. It means to see in pictures and images.

That's how our mind works – by seeing *PICTURES* and images. Why not take a few moments now and send yourself a *PICTURE* of the "you" that you want to be, having and experiencing what you want to have and experience.

Trust me, it won't be a waste of time.

PICTURE PERFECT!

CHAPTER 10
Broadcast, Project, and Radiate What You Desire

The Word of God tells us, *"As a man thinks in his heart – so is he"* (Proverbs 23:7). The word *"heart"* in this verse could be translated and maybe should have been translated as *"mind."*

You can investigate this word by looking at Strong's Concordance #5314. It is the Hebrew word, "Nephesh," and it is translated as both "heart" and "mind" throughout the Old Testament. The way you think of yourself in your heart and *Picture* yourself in your mind is the way that God and life will treat you.

What your mind *Pictured* you would be and have – you have now become and now possess. What your mind *Pictures* you will be in the future – you will become.

Because you will be in the future what you *Picture* yourself to be today, it is essential that you start at once sending yourself *Mental Photographs* and *Videos* of who you want to become and what you want to have and experience in the days ahead.

Because so much of our thinking involves the mental pictures we form in our mind and view regularly, for this study, I will paraphrase what God said in Proverbs 23:7 and I will say, "The *MENTAL PHOTOS* a man creates and views regularly – will determine what he becomes and has!"

The reason why there is still unhappiness and poverty in this universe of lavish abundance is that so many people still do not understand the basic laws of life. *What a man thinks in his mind, so he is. What a man thinks he can have, so he has. What a man thinks he can do, so he can do.* God said so in Proverbs 23:7.

The opposite of those statements are also true. On the negative side: What a man thinks he can't have, he won't have. *What a man thinks and believes he can't do, he won't even try.*

Over one hundred years ago, Henry Ford stated this great truth from Proverbs 23:7. He said, *"Whether you think you can or think you can't – you're right."*

Broadcast, Project, and Radiate What You Wish to Receive from Life

You may have not yet realized that you must broadcast or project or radiate (call it what you will) what you desire in order to attract it into your life. Jesus said, *"Give and it shall be given back to you, good measure, pressed down, shaken together, and running over"* (Luke 6:38).

Jesus was saying that *WHATEVER WE GIVE* would come back to us with increase! We usually think of *GIVING* in terms of money or good works. But there's more, much more! Perhaps you've never thought of *GIVING* in terms of your attitude, your state of mind, or the thoughts you think. These things that you have never thought of in terms of *GIVING* are what you are broadcasting and *GIVING-OUT* continually.

Your attitude, state of mind, thoughts, and the mental pictures you create – are what you are *GIVING* into the invisible creative realm around you, and therefore, they are what you are creating in your life – with increase (Luke 6:38).

Broadcast and give out good thoughts and attitudes and good will come back to you – with increase. Broadcast and give out negative thoughts and attitudes and negative things will come into your life – with increase.

God Does Not Only Multiply Physical Things Back to You

What Jesus was referring to, and what you are capable of *GIVING*, is not just limited to things of physical substance like money. In the verses prior to Luke 6:38, Jesus said that if you *GIVE* mercy, you will receive mercy back to you – with increase. He instructed you to stop *GIVING* judgment to others so that you wouldn't be judged. He said to stop *GIVING OUT* condemnation so that exoneration would come back to you – with increase. He said to *GIVE* forgiveness so that you would receive forgiveness – with increase.

It was after referring to nonphysical things (Luke 6:36-37) that Jesus said to give and that it would be given back to you with increase. Whatever it is that you are giving, whether it is physical or nonphysical, positive or negative, is what will come back to you – with increase. This means that thoughts of abundance and blessings can cause physical abundance and blessings to come back into your life – with increase.

That's Super Great News!

That's super great news because from this day forward you can consciously and deliberately start *GIVING* both physical and nonphysical, beneficial things that will come back to you multiplied, increased, and purposed to enhance your life.

What I'm trying to get believers everywhere to understand is that *"We are WHERE we are because we are WHAT WE ARE and we are WHAT WE ARE because of what we habitually think about and the pictures we constantly create and view in our mind."*

God said, *"As a man thinks in his heart (mind), so is he."* I want you to get excited, realizing that the things you desire can and will be accomplished if they can be first accomplished in your mind.

Your mind is your God-given creative power for good. Your mind is the connecting link between the visible and the invisible. Your mind has been given to you to help you receive what you desire from God and life. Although you were never taught the role that your mind plays in receiving from God in school and you were probably never taught that in church either, God designed you that way.

The ball is in your court. God has given you authority to have what you desire in life. But you must take and use that authority and dare to subdue, change, and reform your world. It all starts by creating and clearly

PICTURING what you want in your mind.

Realize that whatever thoughts and pictures you send yourself; whatever you center your attention upon, steadily, consistently, and deliberately, is what you will create and experience in your life. That's the way that the creative laws of God work for all mankind. Think it. *IN-VISION* it. Give positive action towards it. Experience it.

When you come to the full realization of this truth, your life will become simpler, easier, and more richly satisfying. Instead of struggling and fighting with outside circumstances, why not quietly go to work on your thinking, as God intended, to create the images of what you wish to become, have, and experience in your life.

Since you can have the tangible (house, car, job, money) and the intangible equivlence (love, joy, peace, happiness, confidence, and purpose) of whatever you dare to choose, it's important to *IN-VISION*, to mentally entertain, and to project only what you desire to actually receive in life.

PICTURE PERFECT!

CHAPTER 11
Jacob's Picture Produced...

Jacob was the grandson of Abraham, the son of Isaac and Rebecca. As the story of Jacob unfolds, we see that Jacob cheated his brother out of his inheritance. At his mother's urging, Jacob fled for his life from the wrath of his brother, Esau. Rebecca instructed Jacob to go live with and work for her brother in Haran (Genesis 27:42-43). Once there, he fell in love.

After Jacob began working for his uncle in the land of Haran, something surprising happened to him. He reaped an unhappy result; his uncle Laban cheated him, yet it proved to be a part of a process of increase that would cause him to prosper.

When Jacob met with his uncle, his uncle asked,

"What shall your wages be?" Jacob replied, *"I will serve you for seven years if you let me marry Rachel, your youngest daughter"* (Genesis 29:15-18). They agreed on the wages and Jacob went to work for his uncle, believing that he would soon be with the woman he loved. Yet, he was deceived and found himself married to Leah, Rachel's older sister.

Jacob's uncle deceived him by switching daughters. Jacob found it was necessary to work seven additional years for the girl of his dreams, Rachel. In addition to that, the Bible says that his uncle changed his wages ten times.

It seems that Jacob was reaping the evil he had previously sown in his younger days. He had cheated his own brother and others in the past; now he was being cheated in return.

Jacob, being a direct descendent from Abraham, still had the promise from God that he would receive the blessing of Abraham, which included great prosperity. But at the time, it certainly did not look like his covenant of prosperity was working. Instead of working for money and getting rich, he had to work fourteen years for the girl with whom he was in love.

When you meet disappointing experiences constructively and in faith, God will make a way for you to be able to go forward into greater blessings.

That's what happened to Jacob. Like Jacob, the blessing of Abraham belongs to you, too. *"And because you belong to Jesus Christ, you are now Abraham's seed and heirs according to the promise"* (Galatians 3:29).

Instead of crying, whining, and complaining, *"This is a terrible injustice,"* *"I have been cheated,"* *"I'm so bummed out,"* and *"I don't even know if I can go on,"* simply know that Better Days Are Ahead for you and that by *IN-VISIONing* what you desire, by faith and consistency, what you desire must come into your possession.

Never Waste Time and Energy Fighting the Present Disappointments!

Never waste time and energy fighting the present disappointments. If you do, you will get bogged down in failure. Trusting God for the increase, Jacob paid his uncle Laban fourteen years of labor in exchange for both Leah and Rachel.

Jacob Pictured Himself Prosperous

Years later, Jacob asked for a financial settlement

from his uncle because he wanted to return to his homeland. His uncle did not want to free him because the blessing of God on Jacob's life was making Laban rich (Genesis 30:26-30).

Laban finally agreed to a financial settlement and asked Jacob what he thought fair compensation would be for making him rich. Jacob told his uncle that all he wanted was all the speckled and spotted goats and sheep that would be born in Laban's flocks, so that he could start his own flocks and began to realize financial independence.

Laban agreed that Jacob could have all the future speckled and spotted goats and sheep that were born from his flocks. He was willing to make this agreement because very few of the goats and sheep in his flocks and herds were spotted or speckled and it was very unlikely that their offspring would be spotted and speckled.

It soon became apparent that Laban had no intention of sharing his livestock with Jacob, though in reality, he had to acknowledge that it was Jacob that had made him rich. Instead, Laban secretly ordered the spotted female animals removed from the herd, leaving only the plain (non-spotted) ones, which he assumed would naturally reproduce only plain goats and sheep.

To keep from being cheated out of what was rightfully his, Jacob used the *Picturing Power* of his mind to change the situation. He Pictured Perfectly what he desired. You can do that, too. Jacob *IN-VISIONed* (sent himself a picture) that he had a huge herd of spotted and speckled goats and sheep.

While in the process of *IN-VISIONing* himself with a huge flock, God gave him an idea. Be confident that what God did for others, He wants to, and will do for you.

Jacob took fresh poplar rods (tree branches) and peeled away some of the bark, causing white streaks in them. He placed these streaked rods in the watering troughs and around where the flocks conceived; they brought forth ring-streaked, speckled goats and sheep. Jacob *IN-VISIONed* what he wanted and forced the goats and sheep to *SEE* themselves as he saw them when they came to drink water and mate: ring-streaked and speckled.

Jacob set a *Picture* around the herd of what he desired, not only for himself to see, but for the cattle to see, also. Jacob proved that you can *Picture* your desire and have it quietly come to you regardless of what others around you are saying or doing. Jacob increased his uncle's flocks first, in order to be able to marry Rachel, and then he increased his own flocks through the power of *IN-VISIONing*.

He reminded his uncle, *"You had a little flock before I came. And now it has increased and multiplied into a multitude, and the Lord has blessed you since my coming"* (Genesis 30:30).

When your blessing, that is, what is rightfully yours is withheld from you, instead of fighting, arguing, or trying to reason with anyone to make them give you what you deserve, just get a Perfect Picture of the results you desire and look at that picture daily.

As Jacob proved, you can create a *Mental Image* of your blessing and bring it into your possession without trying to reason through it or resorting to underhanded methods to get it.

Mental Imaging or *IN-VISIONing* was a well-known success technique among the ancient people, but has been lost in our generation.

Because *Picturing* what you desire and keeping what you desire before your eyes is scriptural, I want to revive that powerful principle of God so that we, the Body of Christ, can start demonstrating God's amazing, supernatural results.

The wealth that Jacob acquired through the Perfect Picturing Power of the mind is described in Genesis 30:43. The Bible says, *"IN THIS WAY the man grew exceedingly rich and had much cattle, maidservants, man servants, camels, and donkeys."* Please notice that Genesis 30:43 says, *"IN THIS WAY..."* In what way? By *IN-VISIONing* the desired results!

I am confident that you also shall grow exceedingly rich as you stop *IN-VISIONing* what you don't want as you continually *IN-VISION* the powerful new *PICTURES* of what God has promised you and what you do want.

PICTURE PERFECT!

CHAPTER 12
The Nuts and Bolts

If a man were to endeavor to hold his arms straight out, away from his body, his arms would eventually fall to his sides, no matter how much he resisted. By law, gravity pulls his arms down to his sides and eventually his arms will feel so heavy and his muscles will feel so fatigued, he will be unable to hold his arms out.

In like manner, what you end up receiving from God and life is attracted to you by the irresistible force of your thoughts and *Mental Pictures*. In other words, what you *BELIEVE*. Jesus said, *"The way you believe, is how it will be done for you"* (Matthew 8:13, paraphrased).

If you *SEE* yourself unworthy, undeserving, or disqualified because you have blown it in some area, you become incapable of receiving your hearts desire.

If, on the other hand, you *SEE* yourself the way God made you to be *IN-CHRIST*, you are now capable of receiving all that God has for you because Jesus said, *"As you have believed, so be it done unto you."*

Again, I cannot stress enough the need for you to have a *Perfect Picture* of what you want and desire. Just as gravity puts an invisible demand on a man's arms as he endeavors to hold them straight out at his side for any length of time, your *IN-VISION* puts an irresistible demand on the reality of what you are Picturing.

You might say that gravity sends out a signal saying, *"Come to me! Come to me!"* Similarly, your *Perfect Picture* is broadcasting a signal, demanding that what you *SEE* must come to you.

Many people who pray and ask God for big things do not receive what they ask for because they *VIEW* themselves as undeserving and unworthy.

Shame, guilt, and condemnation have blurred the *Picture* making it impossible to conceive or *IN-VISION* what their life would be like were they to accept and really receive what they've asked God for.

People experiencing condemnation can't *IN-VISION* or get a *Perfect Picture* of themselves having and enjoying what God wants them to have.

Their picture is shame-based (distorted and blurred), which, in their mind, disqualifies them from having what God intends. They ask but can't *Imagine* or *Picture* what it would be like to actually have and experience what they have asked for. They can't *SEE* themselves with it.

God and life can only give you as many good things as you can accept and Picture in your own mind.

If You Want Something, But Can't Imagine Having It, You Can't Have It!

Because we are and have the sum total of our dominant *Mental Pictures* (our *IN-VISION*) it is vital that we consciously choose what Mental Images we view. Otherwise, we will unconsciously think about and create *Mental Pictures* of the things we do not want and what we do not want will continue to be our experience. We will simply keep creating and producing what we already have, nothing more and nothing better.

We must stop looking at useless, unproductive, mental re-runs. These re-runs are, many times, unprofitable, previous images that we have created in our mind. *Pictures* of past painful events and disappointments that we keep sending ourselves, not realizing that we are actually recreating what we do not want.

If we want more from God and more out of life, we must start creating new and desirable *Pictures*. What and how we think along with the *Mental Pictures* we review and look at regularly have everything to do with how much we can accomplish and have.

If we are believing God and can See ourselves succeeding, our chances of success is sure. If we think we are believing God for success, but cannot See ourselves as being successful, we will likely never experience our dream.

The rule is, *"If you CANNOT SEE yourself succeeding, the laws that govern success WILL NOT ALLOW you to succeed."* Picture Perfect!

Your Challenge...

Your challenge is this: Stop unconsciously thinking about what you've always thought. Stop unconsciously viewing the same *Mental Pictures* of loss, failure, and disappointment that you've looked at for so many years. Understand that you have programmed those non-heart's-desire *Pictures* into your subconscious mind; they can only keep producing what you've always experienced and nothing more, nothing better.

You must deliberately use your power of choice to create *Mental Images* that will mirror identically the life, lifestyle, and future that you desire. Otherwise, tomorrow will be just like today. It will simply be a re-run of the past, not a new day.

If you don't change what you think about and how you think about it, if you don't create new, exciting, and powerful *Mental Pictures*, your tomorrows will be just like today. In that sense, you won't have a future, just one long today.

You alone are the designer, architect, creator, builder, and sculptor of your tomorrows. What you create and experience is all based on what and how you think, what you believe to be true and what you *IN-VISION*.

Tomorrow is in total agreement, prepared to give you exactly what you design and create with your thoughts, beliefs, words, decisions, and actions, today. That is why you must not wait until tomorrow to get a Perfect Picture of what you want tomorrow.

An *IN-VISION* is a seed planted in your invisible mental universe soon to be seen in the physical universe around you. Decide what you want, give your attention to what you want, and then make the intentional decision to not focus on the things you don't want.

What Is - Versus What Could Be

Most people utilize the majority of their time thinking about what they are observing around them. In other words, the majority of their time is wasted thinking about their circumstances and problems and not thinking about what they desire. Therefore, they get the same results they've always gotten, over and over again.

If the evening news tells you that times are bad, you might begin to send Pictures to yourself about what your life will look like during these bad times. If you only observe what is – if you only think about what is – what is only has power to give you more of what is; it cannot give you what could be.

When you choose to think about and observe the unprofitable *Mental Pictures* of your yesterdays, you give those unprofitable things the power to reproduce in your today. If you are not head-over-heels in love with your life and what you have now, then you must start thinking about and *Perfectly Picturing* something different in order to create something new.

Your current state of affairs is not really who you are today. It is a residual outcome of the thoughts, actions, and Mental Pictures from your past.

Don't define yourself by your current state of affairs or circumstances. To do so is to doom yourself to failure in your future. By creating new *Mental Pictures* and thinking differently today you will change your state of affairs and circumstances tomorrow.

Getting a *Perfect Picture* of your heart's desire is like putting money in the bank and making payments towards what you want until it's fully yours. Let me give you a word of wisdom here. Get out of the mental drama, worrying about when "what you want" will appear. Rest in perfect peace that, like a seed, what you have asked of God and what you have been picturing is in the process of manifesting. Keep the switch of faith turned on, keep viewing your *Perfect Picture* often.

Babies Are Born

In the newspaper's obituary section, every day, you can read about a doctor, dentist, schoolteacher, business owner, mother, or contractor, who died.

When a woman gives birth to a child, do you notice that the doctor right away tells the new mother that she now has either a boy or a girl? The doctor doesn't say, *"Congratulations, you've just given birth to a United States Congressman."* Neither does the doctor say to the mother, *"I'm sorry ma'am, you've just given birth to a total loser."*

The doctor doesn't call the newborn a famous psychiatrist, a future rock star, a multimillionaire businessman, or a criminal. The doctor only states the sex of the newborn — not what the baby will become. Babies are born, but doctors, lawyers, politicians, school teachers, janitors, fry cooks, and even criminals, will one day die.

Something must occur between birth and death that causes a person to become what they end up being. What an individual does and becomes depends on what they think about, based on the *Mental Pictures* they create and on which they focus, and based on the decisions they make, which are usually in harmony with those *Mental Pictures*.

What babies become is largely dependent on the *Pictures* others send to them and they can't help but live out what they've been shown. It will take a brand new set of *Perfect Pictures* for them to change their experience, to shape their future.

CHAPTER 13
Thought Cash – Does It Really Exist?

When negative self-talk, worry, and memories of negative situations are rehearsed and viewed over and over again, they create vivid *Mental Images*; they are then copied onto your mind. Every thought, remembrance, and rehearsal of something negative causes a new, enhanced *Picture* of that discouraging event or feeling to duplicate on your mental hard drive.

The more negative *Mental Pictures*: copies, feelings, and disappointments on the hard drive – the easier it is to retrieve, relive, and re-feel those painful events and the easier it becomes to experience new, similarly painful events.

Doesn't that explain why so many people are unhappy? The needle on their mental record player automatically skips to an unwanted groove on their record and plays something unpleasant, over and over again. In fact, because this negative groove is so deep, that's all it can play.

Let's imagine a scenario in which you were to purchase only one song from iTunes over and over hundreds, even thousands, of times until you filled up your iPod with only one song. This is comparable to what you do in your mind when you habitually worry and continue looking at past disappointing *Mental Pictures.*

You copy and paste the negative images and feelings over and over until your conscious and subconscious mind is so full with copies of the same information that you can't possibly benefit from it. Soon, after so many rewrites and copies of the same harmful information, that's all you easily think about and *Picture* because that's what's in there the most.

Everything you think about becomes tainted and distorted by that recopied information and your perception becomes distorted and perverted. It's only natural, then, that the reality these *Pictures* represent, is all that seems to show up in your life.

The more you worry and talk negatively to yourself, rerunning the same disempowering *Pictures* and scenarios in your mind, the fuller your mental hard drive becomes with the harmful and unproductive information and the easier it becomes to only retrieve, think about, and *Picture* that harmful information.

Avoid Creating Harmful Ghost-Like Images in Your Mind

Years ago, if a television set were left on a paused image from a video game or VCR all day, it would burn a permanent, ghost-like image onto the tube and viewing screen.

You could still watch regular TV, but the ghost of the video game would still be embedded like a shadow in what you saw. In like manner, continuous negative thoughts burn a negative image permanently on the screen of your mind and you become haunted by the ghost of it. Obviously, you can think about other things, but that unwanted image will still be present just under the surface.

On a computer screen desktop there may be a hundred folders designed to contain different information and results, to take you to the Internet, or to open an account file or a word document, etc. However, if every file only has copies of one original file on it and not the promised information in its title, all you can retrieve is what you don't want; you will become unable to receive what you do want.

When you worry and *IN-VISION* (send yourself a picture of) substandard things, you fill every folder on your Mental Desktop with the same harmful information and eventually all you can ever retrieve and experience is something negative. At that point, you can only retrieve and manifest what you would rather not have.

The Bible character, Job, didn't want tragedy and calamity in his life for him or his family. However, he constantly *IN-VISIONed* (sent himself mental photographs) thoughts of evil befalling his kids; soon, it did. In his words, Job admitted, *"The thing I greatly feared and the things I didn't want, have come upon me"* (Job 3:25). We can clearly ascertain that Job had *STINKING THINKING.*

Get Rid of the Stinking Thinking

Recently my middle son, daughter-in-law, and my two beautiful and wonderfully gifted granddaughters were excited about moving into a larger house. When they went to view the house for the first time, it seemed perfect. The girls would each get their own room, which made them feel grown up. The house looked ideal and smelled freshly painted. It also had a beautiful pool that had been a heart's desire of theirs for some time.

They paid no attention to the fact that every window in the house was open and that there were *Glade Room Fresheners* in every room.

Later, when they went to do the final walk-through and pick up the keys, all the windows were closed and they noticed that the house smelled like cigarette smoke. When they questioned the realtor about the foul smell, he admitted that five years ago, when the original owner lived there, he and his wife both smoked. Since the time that the original owners moved out, the carpets and drapes had been changed and the walls were painted, several times.

It is amazing how the stink of cigarette smoke can permeate and pry its way into every crack and crevice in the walls and wood of a house and linger there for so many years. My daughter-in-law had challenging sinus issues; so obviously, they refused to live in the smelly house and decided that was not the house for them.

That's how *stinking thinking* is in our lives. We think it's gone because we haven't seen those images or thought those thoughts for a while, and yet, they linger there, under the surface, waiting to trip us up. That's why it's important to start sending yourself brand-new *PICTURES* of the improved lifestyle you desire.

Stop thinking that other people, things, situations, and circumstances have power to penalize you, slow your progress, or harm you in any way. They don't! Start realizing that nothing can stand between you and the good things you desire if you really believe God and bring your thoughts, words, and Mental Pictures in-line with what you desire and with what God has promised you.

The tenacious character of your old unproductive way of thinking may try to fight you every step of the way as you endeavor to think new thoughts and send yourself new pictures. If you suspect that you still have some stink lingering in the walls and crevices of your mind, make the following affirmation, daily, to be sure that you are building new, powerful, and productive thoughts to replace the old harmful, disempowering thoughts:

I am the rich child of a loving, Heavenly Father. All that the Father has is mine to experience and enjoy. His Divine Wisdom is now showing me how to claim what Jesus has already provided for me. I claim and receive the wealth, health, and happiness that is mine in Christ Jesus. The Spirit of God is now opening the way for my immediate blessings and increase. I see it! I visualize it! I IN-VISION it! I embrace it! I receive it! I have it!

Our Mind is the Cause of Many of the Effects We Experience

We have heard about the *Law of Cause and Effect* when it comes to why stuff happens in a predictable way. We know that the same cause will always produce the same *effect*. In a practical way, we know that it doesn't matter how many times you accidentally put your hand into the fire, it will always burn, *causing* pain as its *effect*, every time. Your hand coming into contact with fire is the *cause* that always produces the *effect* of pain.

What we may not have taken into consideration is that what you *Mentally Picture* on a continuous basis creates a *CAUSE* that always produces a corresponding result or *EFFECT*. The *Laws of Cause and Effect* perfectly reflect back to us, in our experience, the things we think about and *IN-VISION* most often. The *Mental Pictures* we view regularly are the cause of our results. What we view regularly is the *CAUSE*; what we obtain and experience in life is the *EFFECT*.

Ponder on the Glory of God and the Possibilities He Presents to Us

Too often we ponder on our *Mental Pictures* of fear, worry, and limitation rather than the glory of

God and the possibilities He presents to us. If we continually think only according to what we physically *SEE* now transpiring around us, our focus on these images will merely perpetuate the old limitations and disappointments we've experienced in the past.

We must begin to *SEE* through the *"eyes of faith"* and develop *Mental Pictures* of the promises of God proving true in our experience. We should *IN-VISION* our life today as a life more blessed than yesterday. A wonderful new life awaits you as you get in the habit of thinking and perceiving things differently.

The Spirit of God can only give you what you can *SEE* and what you are willing to receive.

God Wants You to Have What He Paid For!

The Children of Israel were not willing to *SEE* themselves as deserving or worthy of the very best land in the world, the Promised Land. They were not willing to take what God had freely provided for them because of their poor self-image, which was the perverted *Inner Picture* they had of themselves. In a very real sense, God did not disqualify them, they disqualified themselves by *PICTURING* wrong things!

How sad that so many Christians today disqualify

themselves from God's best by viewing distorted pictures of shame, unworthiness, and guilt, when the truth is that it's God's deepest desire to give them His best.

Think of it this way: Since God did not withhold the agonies of the whipping post and the cross from His Son Jesus, why would He now withhold from US what those agonies purchased? (See Romans 8:32.) Take hold of God's mighty promises and allow yourself to become a possibility thinker, not an impossibility thinker. Jesus said, *"All things are possible to him that believes"* (Mark 9:23). That's you!

Burn up the old *Mental Pictures* of failure, loss, and disappointment. Create some new *Mental Pictures* of happiness, great health, plenty of money, great relationships with others, and the wonderful life you desire and you deserve.

We must cast off the worry and intellectual doubt, which affirms that things must continue as they have always been. Things don't have to continue the way they've always been for you. Through the power of faith and *IN-VISION*, things can change.

You're about to turn the corner. You're about to get a breakthrough. A new day has dawned for you. *Expect it* and *Picture it* by imprinting that truth onto the canvas of your mind.

Mental Pictures Put What You See on "Layaway"

We think in *Pictures*. Our thoughts create and conceive positive or negative Pictures in our mind. Some department stores permit their customers to put items that they desire to purchase on layaway. *"Layaway"* is a system of paying a deposit to secure an item for later purchase. Usually, money is paid towards that item on a regular basis until it is paid off, at which time you now own it and can take it with you.

When a *Picture* is conceived or developed in our mind, it puts the manifestation of what is *Pictured* on *"Layaway"* in the department store of the universe. Desire, focus, expectancy, *Mental Pictures*, and thoughts given toward any subject, good or bad, are like currency or money being paid towards purchasing that good or bad expectancy.

Thought Cash, Your Unseen Mental Currency

Any continued thought or *Mental Picture*, viewed often, invests *Thought Cash* towards the purchase of what was thought or *Pictured*. When enough *Thought Cash* is paid towards the original thought or *Picture*, what was thought or *Pictured* is eventually purchased and paid in full; it is then delivered to you.

If you saw an expensive pair of shoes in a store that you wanted to buy, and didn't have the money that day to pay for it in full, you might put a deposit on the shoes and bring the remainder of the money in at another time. When you *Mentally Picture* something, giving more thought and observation to that *Picture*, the more assured you can be that you are in the process of purchasing what you've been looking at; you will soon possess what was Pictured.

Fear, doubt, and worry causes you to pay *Thought Cash* towards something you don't want and, in the end, it will surely give you buyer's remorse.

Perhaps you've been unaware of it, but what you *Picture* in your mind has always been the purchasing power for the things you receive in life. There is no getting around this fact. God set life up to work that way.

Your thoughts, feelings, emotions, attitude, and what you *IN-VISION* always notifies the invisible world around you of what you want it to bring your way, what you are purchasing. Thoughts are like cash. They are *spiritual currency* that purchase everything you get, experience, and become. Thoughts, like cash, can obtain great food or cow manure. It's your choice.

If you allow your mind to view and focus on any Picture that just happens to drift into your mind, you create what you get by default. That's how things you don't want just show up "Out of the Blue" and blindside you. The only way to get what you desire in life is to think about and *IN-VISION* only the things you want.

To get what you want in life, trust God; Picture Perfectly what you want.

Cast Down Negative Mental Pictures

God told us to *"Cast down imaginations, reasonings, and every high thing that exalts itself against the knowledge of God, and bring every thought into the obedience of Christ"* (2 Corinthians 10:5). We are instructed to demolish arguments and every pretension that sets itself up against the knowledge of God, to take captive every thought so that it becomes obedient to Christ.

The question is, *"WHY* does God want us to cast those things down?"

Because when you cast down lies, DISEMPOWERING beliefs, unprofitable thoughts, or negative Mental Pictures, you strip those harmful things of their power to materialize in your life.

Things that are *CONTRARY* to God and His will for your life have the power to manifest in your life and become your experience if you allow them to turn into *Mental Pictures* and beliefs. Imaginations, reasonings, and high things that exalt themselves against the knowledge of God drift into your mind with an agenda. Their agenda is to take root, grow, and bear poisonous fruit in your life. Fruit that neither God nor you want.

What you think – materializes. Thoughts become things. Everything we see and use daily came into existence that way. That's the way God designed it. That's the process!

Suppose that in your kitchen you have linoleum flooring. Now suppose that in an adjoining room you have nice new carpet that you're really proud of. What would happen if you were to spill a gallon of grape juice on your linoleum floor near the adjoining room?

One of the first things you might do is take a towel and try to block the juice's access to the carpet because you know that the grape juice will stain and ruin your nice new carpet. Your number one priority is to stop the grape juice from staining your new carpet. In fact, you may be motivated enough to lie down on the floor and use your body as a dam in an effort to stop the juice and protect your carpet.

Since your mind and what you get in life is more

important than carpet, why wouldn't you protect your mind and life from what negative imaginations and *Mental Pictures* will do to your mind and life?

In your act of casting down imaginations and thoughts that try to exalt themselves above what God told you is true, you keep those harmful things from staining your mind and ruining your life.

Where the Disconnect Occurred

Without intentionally doing it, well-meaning people, such as your parents, friends, relatives, teachers, coaches, maybe even pastors, have repeatedly trained you to believe and think in ways that can't possibly produce good results. You have been taught things about God that don't produce what God has promised and intended for you, what Jesus died to purchase for you! How frustrating!

In your personal life, there are many areas that you would swear to God that you are thinking and believing the right way, *IN-VISIONing* right and beneficial things. However, you are mistaken. The Bible says, *"Every way of a man is right in his own eyes,"* Proverbs 21:2. So here's the test. If it's not producing good results, God results, it cannot be the way God intends it.

In life, and in the things of God, it does not matter if you're a really good person, mean well, and your intentions are noble. If you think, believe, and Picture wrong things and you misuse natural and spiritual laws, you must bear the consequences.

If the way you currently think and the Pictures you have been sending to yourself and viewing daily were capable of producing what you desire – you would already have what you desire.

In order for you to get different results, you have to do something different, and *IT ALWAYS STARTS WITH YOUR THINKING.*

CHAPTER 14
Breaking Your Self-Imposed Limitations

The Olympic Games originated in the eighth century B.C. and were held in Olympia, Greece. Today, approximately two hundred countries participate in the modern Olympic Games, held in various countries all around the world every four years. But, even before the Olympic Games, men and women have been competing to see who ran the fastest.

Since the beginning of modern timekeeping, athletes have endeavored to take seconds, fractions of a second, off of the time clock as they ran various distances.

The competition has always been fierce, regardless of the length of the race. There was a day when the thought of running a mile in less than four minutes seemed inconceivable, completely unattainable, because the feat would severely punish the body. Even though runners were super strong and gifted athletes, their coaches, mentors, and role models put within their minds the *FACT* that no one would ever be able to run a mile in less than four minutes.

The medical profession, scientists, and the common sense belief of world-renowned athletes were persuaded that to put that type of strain on a human body would cause the heart to burst. Medically, scientifically, and practically, it was thought impossible to run a mile in less than four minutes.

By the early 1950s, several prominent runners were coming close to the sub-four-minute mile mark, only nine or ten seconds over four minutes.

After his clear defeat in the 1952 Olympics, long distance runner Roger Bannister spent two months deciding whether he should give up running altogether.

Instead of giving up, he set for himself a new goal: to be the first man ever to run a mile in under four minutes. He *IN-VISIONed* it done and, more importantly, he *IN-VISIONed* himself as the one who would accomplish it. Up until this time, Bannister only trained moderately for his events. Now, because he changed his inner *Picture*, he began training more intensively.

On May 2, 1953, he made an attempt to break the British record. Banister ran a mile in four minutes, 3.6 seconds. He said, *"This race made me realize (IN-VISION) that the sub-four-minute mile was not out of reach."*

On May 6, 1954, in England, at an Oxford University track meet, Dr. Roger Bannister stunned the sports world when he became the first man ever to run a mile in less than four minutes. Bannister's time was three minutes, 59.4 seconds.

Forty-six days later, John Landy, from Australia, beat his record, proving that the four-minute-mile was a mental ceiling, not a physical impossibility. Within the next year, dozens of athletes ran the mile in less than four minutes. Since 1954, thousands have.

What Were They Thinking?

Imagine the audio, video tapes, and Pictures that were heard and watched in the minds of the greatest athletes in the world when they stepped into the starting blocks before a race. Perhaps they thought something like, *"I've been training really hard and I know I'm in excellent shape. I also know that the experts told me I would be harming my body, that I may even be risking my life if I push myself so hard that I come close to the four-minute-mile. I will definitely do my best, try to win the race, but forget about the possibility of breaking the four-minute-mile mark."*

Whatever it was that the runners thought about and *Pictured* in their minds, it was certainly something that had been placed there by impossibility thinkers, the Experts!

We can do a play on words with the word, "EXPERT." The word expert is a compound word, made up of two individual words. "EX" means "former," or "used to be." The word, "PERT" means "Jaunty, cheerful, saucy, lively, and in good health."

Stop listening to the experts. You don't want someone who used to be cheerful, saucy, and lively, telling you what you can and cannot do, do you? What are you *NOT* attempting because someone else said you shouldn't even try or because you have your own, self-imposed, limiting beliefs?

Remember, running a mile in less than four minutes was a mental ceiling and not a physical impossibility that plagued the minds of thousands of athletes for thousands of years. The fact is that breaking the four-minute-mile would still be an impossibility had not one man deliberately *IN-VISIONed* that he could do it.

God wants you to take on the mindset that *"I (meaning YOU!) can do all things through Christ who strengthens me"* (Philippians 4:13).

Satan Comes to Deceive the Whole World

Satan's purpose is to steal, to kill, and to destroy. He does this through deception (John 10:10 with Revelation 12:9). Maybe he is belittling your life by deceiving you into thinking things like...

> You are unworthy of God's best.
> You don't qualify for blessings.
> It's not God's will for you to live your dream.
> It's not God's will for you to be rich.
> You don't deserve true happiness.
> Life's a struggle.
> Money doesn't come to you easily.
> It's hard to make ends meet.
> Your life is too screwed up for you to succeed.
> God wants you to be poor and sick.
> Poverty is your lot in life, your fate.

NO! ALL THAT KIND OF THINKING IS DECEPTION! IT'S CRAP!!!

Who spoke into your life, in your past, that's causing your today to be "Belittled?" When I speak of being

Belittled I'm often referring to stuff that you were told by your parents, family members, teachers, friends, enemies, coaches, and maybe even your pastors.

Well-meaning people with the greatest of intentions have spoken things into your life that have caused your life to be less, often much less, than God desired and intended it to be.

God's purpose and my purpose for writing this book is for you to *Be-More*, not to *Be-Little* or *Be-Less*.

It's time to get rid of that garbage-dump thinking that has never benefited you in any way and start Picturing yourself the way God sees you. God sees you as a winner, a champion, more than a conqueror, the apple of His eye, the beloved of the Lord, His workmanship created in Christ Jesus, and an ambassador from heaven.

It's time for you to catch the vision, God's vision. You do that by *IN-VISIONing* yourself the way God sees you.

You do that by *Picturing Perfectly* who God made you to be.

CHAPTER 15
If It's Alive – It's Meant To Thrive!

It is important for you to *visualize* and feel that you are becoming more successful and that you are helping others to do so, also. Abundance is a *feeling*. Be more deliberate to include the feeling of abundance when you look at your *Picture* of abundance.

Because you now know that you are finally on the right track, your every act, the tone of your voice, your looks should express a quiet, rich assurance of success and abundance. Trying to convince others of your success is not necessary when you get the feeling of richness implanted in your *Mental Photo Album*. Where it is then radiated from you to God and subconsciously communicated to others.

As you practice *"acting the way you SEE yourself*

becoming" on a regular basis, you will become aware that other people want to be associated with you because they are subconsciously aware of the benefits of being in your presence and doing business with you.

Just by quietly working to get the mindset and feeling of richness, happiness, success, and prosperity, you will draw to yourself prosperous-minded people whom you have never seen before; they will become your customers, associates and friends.

People are naturally and unconsciously drawn to an atmosphere of increase. All of life is seeking increase. God designed *EVERYTHING*, and I do mean *EVERYTHING* He created to want to become more. As you think of yourself, Picture yourself, and allow yourself to feel prosperous, you will start conveying the impression of increase to other people and they will want to be associated with you.

As you give thought and image to increase and quietly, in the deep recesses of your own mind, create *High-Definition Mental Photos* of the life you wish to live and the blessings you wish to share with others, people will be attracted to you, not just to receive from you, but they'll also automatically want to help you succeed.

Dare to invoke God's *Laws of Increase* in every way you possibly can by holding the thought and *Picture* of increase in everything you do and with everyone you meet.

The whole tide of your thinking is turning from failure to success, from lack to abundance, from sickness to health, from curse to blessing, and it won't be long until you experience the great new things that you have been *IN-VISIONing*.

God Never Runs Out of Resources

The spiritual substance from which all visible wealth and riches come can never be depleted. There is enough for everyone. No one has to do without in order for you to have more and you don't have to do without for others to have more.

God's rich supply is with you all the time. It responds to your faith in it and your demands upon it. God's unfailing resource is always ready to give. Pour your images of abundance and words of faith into the creative substance of God and you will prosper no matter how the economy or your current circumstance looks.

Turn the divine energy of your thinking into *Pictures* of increase and you will have plenty of abundance regardless of what people around you are saying, doing, and experiencing.

It matters not what other's think about you and your future; what matters is what *YOU* think about *YOU* and your future. Others have no power over you; so don't let their negative thoughts become your problem. Stay the course!

You are in the world, but you are not of the world (John 17:16). You are operating with laws and principles that the average man knows nothing about. You are lavishly provided for by the inexhaustible resources of God. *Picture That!*

Use your God-given, creative power of thought and imagination to *IN-VISION* prosperity by concentrating your thoughts, feelings, relationships, and activities on prosperity, not failure or lack. Expect to become prosperous and start thinking, *Picturing*, and speaking in those terms at all times.

Break the Chains of Petty Thinking

Nobody can keep your success and prosperity from you – no one but you, alone. God has endless doors of success, opportunities, and blessings ready to open for you if you'll just *Picture* it, believe it, and act appropriately and in faith when it presents itself.

There is plenty of success and prosperity for all.

Many people are confused about the correct spiritual attitude towards money. It's important that you spend time thinking about prosperity. What you think about is what you bring about. There is nothing wrong with money or with you wanting more of it. Money is a God-given medium of exchange and there is nothing evil about that.

The moment we let go of all the wrong ideas that someone ignorantly taught us many years ago – that money is evil – we find that money circulates in our financial affairs much more easily.

Perhaps you wonder why it's important to cultivate a favorable attitude about money in order to attract it. Well, money is filled with the intelligence of the universe, from which it was created. Money reacts to our attitudes about it, almost as if it were a living thing.

American currency has a statement on it, which says, *"In God we trust."* Since you trust in God also, you and money are in agreement. Money trusts in God and you trust in God. Therefore, you are compatible with money and should have plenty of it.

Since the *Law of Gratitude* states that you attract whatever you appreciate, and repel whatever you despise, money responds accordingly. If you think favorably about money and *Picture* all of the wholesome and beneficial things you can do with it, you multiply and increase it into your life.

The Image Makes the Condition

If you feed your imagination halfhearted, lukewarm, and vague *Mental Pictures*, those are the kinds of results you will get. It requires strong, emotional, passionate, and vivid *Mental Pictures* to make the right impression on the creative power of God.

Remember, Jesus said, *"What things soever you DESIRE when you pray believe that you receive them, and you shall have them"* (Mark 11:24). Notice that Jesus used the word *"DESIRE."* He didn't say, *"What things soever you prefer, wish for, or think would be nice."* NO. He said *DESIRE.*

"Desire" is a strong word with strong meaning; desire is a mental state you must develop and remain in, in order to materialize what you want.

Since anything less than passionate desire will not be satisfactory in starting the creative process, anything less will require you to start all over again. Therefore, incorporate passion and desire into your *Mental Pictures* in the beginning and save yourself double work.

Truly, the image does make the condition, but it's up to you to make the image look the way you want it to look. Get busy and quietly imagine (*Picture*) what you desire in full detail as you wish it to be when it materializes. It is true that man becomes what he imagines himself to be. God said, *"As a man thinks in his heart, so is he"* (Proverbs 23:7).

Your continuous, passionate, prosperous, desirable, and possibility-filled thoughts and your purposeful and vivid *Mental Pictures* are sufficient to remove the unwanted conditions in your life and create anything that you desire.

The word *"Affirm"* means to *"make firm."* Through verbal affirmations and declarations, declare the blessings from God and life that you want. Instead of continually talking about what you don't want, begin to *"make firm"* in your mind the good things you desire. As you continue to affirm the desired blessings and *Picture* them with clarity, they rush towards you as visible results.

That being true – *Picture Perfect!*

CHAPTER 16
God Wants YOU Rightly Rich!

As I minister to leaders, pastors, and the wonderful people of God in the Body of Christ, one of the most startling and disappointing observations I make is that the vast majority still try to resolve the old conflict of whether or not they should desire prosperity. Nearly everyone attending church wants to be prosperous, whether they admit it or not; they prove it every day by going to work.

Every pastor and leader wants to be prosperous so that they can fulfill the vision God gave to them and help a multitude of people.

The conflict is that, secretly, they wonder whether or not they should seek wealth and riches or whether those aspects of prosperity are forbidden or evil, and would be almost like seeking the occult, in God's eyes.

Most Christians seem to feel guilty about wanting to be prosperous, though, of course, they work hard every day on the job to become more prosperous. Obviously, the question still brings a battle to their mind as to whether or not prosperity is sinful and poverty is virtuous.

The mental struggle in their thinking concerning whether or not being wealthy is, or isn't, the will of God, has set up inconsistent results in their lives, neutralizing their effort to succeed, no matter how hard they work.

It seems to me that the majority of people work extremely hard to get ahead, but what they desire always seems just out of reach. Wonderful Christian people and even church leaders seem quite confused about whether prosperity should be considered a spiritual blessing or whether it is a distracting curse.

Over the years, I have found that the most common cause of failure in believers is this conflicting idea about whether success is divinely ordained or divinely damned.

When coming to me for counsel concerning insufficiency and lack in their lives, I have found that the common false belief in the Body of Christ is that failure and lack are more spiritually approved by God than success, since riches are regarded as an object of worship or a *"false god"* by the religious multitude.

It seems that every conflicted person is steeped in the false belief that *"Money is the root of all evil"* (1 Timothy 6:10). That's not what this verse says!

It's extremely interesting to me that Christian's incorrectly quote this verse so often when that's not what the verse says at all. It says, *"The LOVE of money is the root of all evil."* Obviously, whether you're rich or whether you're poor, you could love money in a way that God didn't intend, thereby worshipping it as a god. Loving money in an inappropriate way can lead to all manners of crime, even murder.

Someway, somehow, people who are supposed to enjoy the benefits that money can provide and promote the kingdom of God by supporting the preaching of the gospel *IN-VISION* all sorts of negative abuses and misuses of money. They totally throw the baby out with the bathwater.

I want you to get creative and start *IN-VISIONing* all sorts of beneficial things you can do as God prospers you.

> **Using Money as a Tool for Good is God's Original Intention for Money**

What those desiring prosperity must understand is that wealth and riches are tools, given as a gift from God to bless your life and enable you to do well on this earth. Being success-minded and prosperity-minded is not serving a false god and those people who view focusing on prosperity and success as serving a false god should stop using God as an excuse for their own laziness and failures.

Adam, Eve, Noah, Abraham, Isaac, Jacob, Joseph, Moses, Joshua, Caleb, David, Daniel, Nehemiah, and even Jesus were one hundred percent success-minded and prosperity-minded.

If a person would sincerely and honestly read through their Bible with a marker and mark every reference to prosperity, wealth, riches, giving, and stewardship, they would soon find that God speaks more about those things than any other subject in the Bible.

The Bible is filled with hundreds of wonderful promises of God regarding prosperity.

Prosperity is your divine heritage. Prosperity is your birthright. As a child of God you should be prosperous, well supplied, and have an abundance of every good thing that pertains to life and godliness (2 Peter 1:4).

Above anything else, your Creator wants you to

prosper (3 John 2). Your Heavenly Father certainly does not have a less noble desire for His children then you have for yours. Your desire to see your children do well is a reflection of the heart of God desiring His children to thrive, succeed, and prosper.

God Wants You to Desire to be Rightly Rich

In order for you to Become More as a man, or a woman, or a Christian, and in order for you *to do more, have more, know more, and help more*, you must have access to many things that will help you develop and grow, things for you to use, ponder upon, interact with, and experience that will improve your skills, talents, and gifting. That requires money.

If I can break it down for you in the simplest of terms, *"Your desire for riches is simply your capacity for a larger life seeking expression and fulfillment."* That which makes you want more money, resources, and opportunities that come alongside is exactly the same thing which makes the plants grow: it is *LIFE* seeking fuller expression.

In my counseling of thousands of believers, including pastors and church leaders, I have discovered that a *poverty-ridden-consciousness* (a mind filled with *Pictures* of lack and insufficiency), is the cause of much misery, family troubles, divorce, and a poor self-image; in many cases, it drives good men and women to drunkenness, prostitution, drugs, addiction, and, in some cases, even suicide.

Today, the Body of Christ needs to be done with thinking *(IN-VISIONing)* that poverty is a virtue. There is no lack, insufficiency, or poverty in God. Why should it exist for the people of God?

Let's face it, you can't be much good to yourself or anyone else unless you are prosperous. Yes, God wants you to be content with what you currently have in that He doesn't want you discouraged and complaining, but He has given you the command and capacity to become more, to thrive, to do well, to succeed, and to increase.

It's not contrary to God's will for you to have big ambitions and want to prosper. Every living thing has the urge of life within it to become *MORE*! Everything God created has the divine urge to become more and increase.

The person who does not desire to be prosperous is abnormal because without prosperity, you live far below your rights and privileges, those that Jesus died to purchase for you.

The first commandment ever given in the Bible was NOT *"Have no other gods before Me"* or *"Love the Lord your God with all your heart and all your soul and all your might."* Rather, the first commandment a human ear ever heard was to become more, thrive, have dominion, and succeed (Genesis 1:26-28). It is therefore of supreme importance that you be prosperous in your physical, mental, spiritual, relational, emotional, and financial realms.

Stop Picturing Insufficiency

Stop *PICTURING* lack and insufficiency. Don't even talk of wanting to be prosperous for the *"good you can do"* in an effort to sound noble. In reality, the good you will do with wealth and riches is secondary. You want to be prosperous mainly because it is your right; it is God's will that you should be prosperous.

God told Abraham, *"I will bless you, and make your name great, and you shall be a blessing"* (Genesis 12:2). God wants to bless you so that you can become a blessing also. I am not discounting this fact. God wants to bless you so that He can establish His covenant with you and through you, according to Deuteronomy 8:18. But primarily, prosperity is your divine heritage as a child of the King, as a son of God, and as His ambassador and representative here on earth (2 Corinthians 5:20).

To state this truth in another way: you should be *RIGHTLY RICH*; God wants you to be rightly rich, not just because of the good you will do with your money, but because of *WHO* you are now that you are *IN-CHRIST* and a child of God.

God isn't poor and He is our loving, Heavenly Father. He is much kinder and has much greater desires for His children to succeed than any earthly parent ever had or ever can have. Get rid of the Satan-inspired, perverted idea that God wants you to sacrifice yourself and do without in order to secure heavenly favor by doing so. God requires nothing of the kind.

Jesus sacrificed Himself and did without in order to secure our heavenly favor with God. There is nothing left for us to do as far as sacrificing and doing without is concerned.

All God expects of us is that we believe and enjoy the full ramifications of His wonderful redemption. What God wants is for you to make the most out of yourself, for yourself and for others. You can help others more by prospering financially and making the most of yourself than in any other way.

The Origin of the False Belief that Poverty is a Virtue

For many years, I wondered why there had been so much talk in the church and so many seemingly inspired and logical messages taught about sacrifice, persecution, doing without, and hard times as necessary phases of the spiritual way of life and pleasing God. Why do so many popular preachers wrongly equate poverty and struggle with spirituality when the Bible says the exact opposite?

Abraham had to have had thousands of servants to be able to arm, equip, and send three hundred and eighteen trained servants, military age, born in his household, to go and rescue his nephew, Lot, from four vicious kings and their armies (Genesis 14:14).

"Abraham was exceedingly rich in sheep, oxen, donkeys, menservants, maidservants, and camels" (Genesis 12:16). And the blessing of Abraham was designed by God to come upon New Testament believers through Jesus Christ (Galatians 3:14). THAT'S YOU!

Before he and Lot separated, they together had so many flocks, herds, and tents that the land was not able to bear them because their substance was so great (Genesis 13:5-6). In addition, the Bible says that,

"Abraham was very rich in silver, cattle, and in gold" (Genesis 13:2); he is called the *"father"* of those of us who have faith (Romans 4 and Galatians 3).

There was a time that I thought and taught that lack, insufficiency, and struggle was the will of God, too. But as I ministered to God's wonderful people and heard heartbreaking stories about the misery that insufficiency causes, I began to seek God about this issue and study the subject diligently.

I found that God clearly wants His people to be blessed in every area of their lives, including their finances. Sometimes it seems like revelation and illumination are like peeling an onion. God begins to open His Word to *YOU* like an onion being peeled one layer at a time until you get to the truth.

How the Body of Christ Came to Accept Poverty as God's Will

As I studied history, I saw that the early church got to the place financially that there was *"no lack among any of the believers"* (Acts 4:34). They corporately experienced supernatural prosperity. *"And with great power the apostles gave witness to the resurrection of the Lord Jesus: and great grace was upon them all, and neither was there any among them that lacked"*

(Acts 4:33-34). *PICTURE THAT!*

They continued to experience Biblical prosperity during the early centuries, but soon Christianity became more secularized, leading to variations and departures from the original teachings of Moses, the Prophets, Jesus, and the Apostles. Eventually, though, the Feudal System (the dominant social system in Europe) during the Middle Ages (from the 5th to the 15th century) made sure that the wealth of various territories and countries was only enjoyed by the privileged few, making peasants out of the masses.

The privileged few made sure that the teaching of *"Poverty and Penance"* was taught systematically to the masses by the churches, as the only way of salvation. They did this in order to keep the people in poverty and make lack and limitations a supposed *"Christian Virtue,"* while leaving more wealth for themselves. The wealthy monarchs, dictators, aristocrats, and warlords of the Middle Ages had found a way to keep the masses utilizing all of their time, strength, and abilities, struggling for a living, all the while thinking that they were pleasing God, but leaving no time, strength, or resources to rebel against the wealthy nobles.

Unsuspecting millions of wonderful people were led to believe that it was *"Saintly and Pleasing to God to be Poor,"* a belief which was useful in preventing revolution among the struggling masses.

Today, I find in the church that those same centuries old, Feudal lies about poverty being a spiritual virtue are as strong as ever.

The very idea and concept that God wants His people struggling and broke is a slap in the face to God. It is a false, Satanic, man-made idea, and certainly not God's rich truth or heritage for His children. If God did not withhold the agonies of the whipping post and the cross from His Son, Jesus, why would He now withhold from us what those agonies purchased?

You should stop *PICTURING* and grappling with the idea of poverty and lack being saintly and embrace the fact that God wants you to prosper. You should stop being conflicted about whether prosperity is a blessing or a curse. Poverty is one of the worst curses known to man and is listed as a curse in Deuteronomy 28:17-20.

Deuteronomy 7:14 gives us a powerful revelation about God's feelings in perhaps the seven most amazing words in the Bible. God said, *"Thou Shall Be Blessed Above All People."* Now that's something to *IN-VISION.*

If prosperity was God's will for His Old Testament people in Deuteronomy, how much more is it His will for His sons and daughters of God, heirs of God, and joint-heirs with Christ Jesus (Romans 8:17) to thrive, be happy, succeed, and prosper today?

Prosperity is a divine desire that should be given divine expression. Prosperity is your divine heritage. Your Heavenly Father's desire is always for your ultimate good. He always wants you to thrive, succeed, and triumph. He never wants you to experience a meager existence. *"It is your Father's good pleasure to give you everything that His kingdom contains"* (Luke 12:32). *PICTURE THAT!*

To Prosper God's Way

To really prosper the way God intends does not mean that you should be satisfied or content with little. No one should be satisfied with little if they are capable of using and enjoying more. Nature's purpose is to advance and develop all life, meaning everyone should have everything they need that contributes to the power, elegance, beauty, development, and richness of life; to be content with less is contrary to God's intent.

For you to prosper pleasures God and fulfills His purpose for you! (Psalm 35:27.)

A desire for riches is really the desire for a richer, fuller, and more abundant life and that desire is praiseworthy. Jesus Himself said, *"I have come that you might have life, and that you might have it more abundantly"* (John 10:10).

Any believer who does not want enough money to buy all that they desire is denying their true *made-in-God's-image* nature and has become un-God-like. Success in life means that you have become what you want to be. Some of the ways that you can become all that you want to be is by traveling, learning, interacting with a variety of people and cultures, and having deep, meaningful, and moving experiences. You can have, do, and experience those things only as you become prosperous enough to afford them.

What Does Love Really Do?

To live fully as God intends, we must love, and love can't be fully expressed through our lives when we are stuck in poverty. For God so loved the world that He GAVE...

Love finds natural and spontaneous expression in giving; our highest happiness is found in providing the blessings and experiences of life to those we love.

People who have nothing to give don't really fill their role as a spouse, as a parent, as a citizen, as a friend, or as a role model for Christ.

You can't properly love others without being *RIGHTLY RICH* because love expresses itself in giving as shown in John 3:16. *"For God so loved the world that He – GAVE – His only begotten Son, that whosoever believes on Him shall not perish, but shall have everlasting life."*

The first thing that Jesus did when He rose from the dead was *"He GAVE gifts unto men"* (Ephesians 4:8). It is perfectly right that you should desire to be rich. That desire is the nature of God inside of you, seeking expression. To neglect the study of how to receive the wealth and riches God provided for you in Christ Jesus is to be derelict in your duty to yourself, to God, and to humanity.

The very highest service you can render to God and humanity is to receive the most you possibly can from God and, in the process, make the most out of yourself. No one can achieve their greatest potential and develop as a person unless they have plenty of money with which to do it.

For us to develop our gifts and talents, we must have use of many tools, do and experience many things, and go many places. Yet, unless we have the money, we can't. A desire for riches is really a desire for a richer, fuller, and more abundant life, and that desire is godly and praiseworthy.

A Snapshot of You

Take a look at your life: your living conditions, the house you live in, the car you drive, the restaurants you eat at, where you vacation, your money in the bank, or the debt you owe. These things reflect your current thinking and tells the rest of us the *Pictures* you've been creating and to which you have been paying attention.

If you want your life to improve, your thinking and beliefs must improve. Jesus said, *"As you have believed, so be it done unto you"* (Matthew 8:13).

So the question is *"What are you believing?"* What unproductive *Pictures* monopolize your time and attention? It's time for a clean slate! If what you're presently believing is not producing what you desire, it's time to flip the script and start taking and viewing new snapshots of your heart's desire and what God has actually promised for your life.

Outward success, happiness, and wealth are the manifestations of your inward thoughts, beliefs, and your current self-image. Those things can only be changed by *Picturing* something different and something better. Your outward manifestations are only a reflection of what's going on within.

For that reason, *Picture Perfect.*

CHAPTER 17
Don't Ask God For Small Things – Thinking Small is Easier

Perhaps you've heard or read about the late Christian Evangelist, George Müller (1805-1898). As a young man, he was a known thief, liar, gambler, and drunk. By the age of ten, he was stealing government money from his father. While his mother was dying, George, at fourteen years of age had an alcohol addiction.

Yet, once he received Jesus as his Lord and Savior, he started *IN-VISIONing* life differently and then, everything changed. He became a man of faith, purpose, compassion, determination and love.

Upon arriving in Bristol, England, he was appalled when he discovered hundreds of orphans abandoned and living in pitiful conditions in the back alleys. Faith arose in his heart and he knew he was destined to do something to change the lives of those children.

No Longer the Problem, But Now the Solution

As a Christian, he *PICTURED* himself as part of the solution, and no longer the problem. He *IN-VISIONed* himself establishing orphanages for the children, providing them with a first class education, teaching them how to live by faith, and training them in the things of God.

Müller never made requests for financial support, nor did he ever go into debt, even though the homes he established to care for the children cost hundreds of thousands of dollars in the 1800s. He *IN-VISIONed* and believed that God would supply his every need. And God did.

Müller tapped into the supernatural power that comes from believing God and *IN-VISIONing* what you desire.

As you embrace and internalize what I'm sharing with you in this book, you too will tap into the supernatural power that comes from believing God and *IN-VISIONing* what *YOU* desire.

Many times, Müller received unsolicited food donations only minutes before they were needed to feed the children, further strengthening his faith in God. For example, on one well-documented occasion, he had the children sit at the breakfast table and give thanks to God for breakfast, even though there was no food on the table and nothing to eat in the house. And sure enough, God supplied.

As the children finished praying, the town baker knocked on the door with sufficient bread to feed everyone. The baker was as surprised as the children were. Somehow, the baker's oven had supernaturally multiplied the bread that morning and he ended up with a double portion.

Perhaps Müller didn't know it at the time, but he was teaching the orphans how to *IN-VISION* supply when in reality, there was none.

Unusual miracles occurred for Müller on a regular basis as he made it his practice to *IN-VISION* himself and the children bountifully provided for by the inexhaustible supply of God.

You should have a similar *Picture* of provision in your mind at all times. Müller's records showed that he traveled over two hundred thousand miles throughout Europe, preaching the gospel, before aviation could aid him in travel; this high of a mileage was an incredible feat in and of itself.

By *IN-VISIONing* God as a loving, caring, and generous Heavenly Father, he was able to care for ten thousand and twenty-four orphans in his lifetime. He also established one hundred and seventeen schools, which offered Christian education to more than one hundred and twenty thousand children, many of them orphans.

Expect Great Things From God And Great Things You Will Have

George Müller has been described as a man of faith to whom God gave millions of dollars (again, back in the 1800s). He has also been called a Prince of Prayer, because of his policy and habit of asking God for what he needed rather than speaking to people about his needs.

Brother Müller once said that the greatest fault of most of us is that we do not ask big enough and we do not continue in prayer (by *visualizing* what we have asked for) until it comes. He also advised others, *"Expect great things of God and great things you will have."*

To add to that excellent statement, I might say, *"IN-VISION great things from God and great things you will have."* He once told a friend, *"I have praised God many times when He sent me ten cents, and I have praised him when he sent me sixty thousand dollars."*

"By faith Moses left Egypt, not fearing the king's anger. He overcame every obstacle because he SAW Him who is invisible" (Hebrews 11:27). Moses conquered all enemies and overcame every obstacle because he *Pictured* God being with him. He must have sent himself *Pictures* of God coming through for him no matter what he faced. You should do the same. You *MUST* do the same, if you want to acquire what you really desire.

Picture Perfectly that God is with you, God is for you, and God is making a way for you even where there is no way. Just like Moses and Brother Müller did, attempt something that is much larger than you are, knowing that God will help you each step of the way.

PICTURE THAT!

CHAPTER 18
The Man Who IN-VISIONed the Future

When we think of famous inventors and visionaries of the past, usually high on the list are names including Benjamin Franklin, Henry Ford, and Thomas Edison. We know that inventors must be able to *IN-VISION* things that do not currently exist. They have to be able to *SEE* things that others have never seen. Inventors must *IN-VISION* in order to invent.

In a sense, I'm asking you to become an inventor and start *SEEING* and *IN-VISIONing* things in your life that do not currently exist, events that you have never experienced before. Perhaps you have never been able to *SEE* yourself as friendly and outgoing, as slim and trim, as living in a nice house, as having plenty of money, as taking your family on great vacations, or whatever. You are in the process of acquiring the tools and principles necessary to obtain the things you could never *SEE* yourself doing or having before.

Just like the inventor has to *IN-VISION* what he desires in order to create it, I want you to begin to *IN-VISION* the blessed life that you want to create. I want to tell you a fascinating story about one scientist who had possibly the greatest ability to *IN-VISION* that the world has ever known. Trust me here, I'm not getting side-tracked; I'm only endeavoring to show you the power of *IN-VISIONing* and I assure you that same power is available to you.

When we think of electricity, we think of Thomas Edison. Edison invented a form of delivering electricity called *Direct Current*. Today, *Direct Current, "DC,"* is how we power portable electronics and toys, by using batteries. Most of us are unaware that the electricity we use every day to power our lights, appliances, and cities, is *Alternating Current, "AC,"* a system of delivery invented by Nikola Tesla, not Thomas Edison.

Recently, I watched the History Channel's four-part docudrama of the *"Men Who Built America,"* and Nikola Tesla was mentioned. I became interested in this man, whom I had never heard anythinng about, apart from the glass globe with the inner element that shoots cool looking lightening-like arcs of electricity in it, called the *"Tesla Coil."*

My interest turned into fascination as I read about Tesla (1856-1943) on *Wikipedia* and later read a *Kindle* book from *Amazon* called *"Imagination and the Man that Invented the 20th Century"* by Sean Patrick. Patrick's book credited Nikola Tesla as *"The Inventor of the Twentieth-Century."* Now, that is a high and lofty title, if you ask me. Let's find out about that guy.

Tesla IN-VISIONed Radio, Fax Machines, and Cell Phones

Before 1900, Tesla said it *WILL* be possible for a businessman in New York to dictate instructions and have them instantly appear in type at his office in London or elsewhere. Tesla predicted that soon people would be able to call and talk to any telephone subscriber on the globe, wirelessly.

Tesla said that an inexpensive instrument, not bigger than a watch, will enable its bearer to hear anywhere, on sea or land, music or songs, the speech of a political leader, the address of an imminent man of science, or the sermon of an eloquent clergyman delivered in some other place thousands of miles away.

Tesla *IN-VISIONed* that any picture, character, drawing, or printed page could be transferred from one place to another place, wirelessly, and that millions of such devices could be operated at the same time. He said that more important than all of this, however, would be the transmission of electric power, without wires, to everyone on earth, free of charge.

Tesla was actually in the process of creating a tower that could wirelessly send electricity anywhere in the world, free of charge. It was Tesla's desire to convince the powerful multimillionaire, J.P. Morgan, to invest in his project so he would have the funds to complete it and bless people.

Tesla explained that his tower could be used for more than transmitting radio signals. He claimed it could be used to saturate the entire globe with electricity, harmless to living things; that anyone and everyone could obtain free electricity from the air or by simply sticking wires into the soil.

Tesla IN-VISIONS and Sends Electricity, Wirelessly

At one point, before 1900, Tesla had a laboratory in Colorado Springs, Colorado, where he successfully lit two hundred lamps from a distance of over twenty-five miles, wirelessly. He proved beyond a shadow of a doubt that electricity could be transmitted effectively at a great distance through the air, without harming human beings.

J.P. Morgan carefully considered Tesla's words and what he had proven; he coldly replied, *"If anyone can draw on the power, where do we put the meter?"* He then refused Tesla's request for more money, forcing Tesla to use his own funds, of which Morgan knew to be insufficient to complete the project.

Undaunted, though, Tesla approached other potential investors, mainly John Jacob Astor, hoping to provide free electricity, wirelessly, to everyone on earth. No one was interested because no money could be made from providing free wireless electricity to everyone on earth.

In 1904, under the pressure that was put on the government by wealthy magnates that didn't want Tesla's plans for his inventions to succeed, the U.S. Patent Office, stripped Tesla of his radio patents and awarded them to Italian inventor, Guglielmo Marconi.

Marconi had used radio technology pioneered by Tesla, eleven years earlier, to transmit the letter "S" in Morse Code over two thousand miles, which insured him financial backing from J.P. Morgan, Thomas Edison, and the steel baron, Andrew Carnegie, all of whom hated Tesla and held sway in every level of government. Marconi was awarded the Nobel Prize in 1911 for his "Achievements in Radio" and was hailed as the "Father of Radio."

After the outbreak of World War I, in 1917, the U.S. government was looking for a way to detect German U-boats and put Edison in charge of finding a workable method. It was Tesla, however, that proposed the use of radio waves to detect the submarines – the first description of radar. Edison rejected the idea as ludicrous.

The world had to wait nearly two decades before Emile Girardeau would develop an Obstacle Locating Radio Device, *"conceived according to the principles stated by Tesla,"* as Girardeau put it.

Tesla IN-VISIONS the Modern Harrier Jump-Jet

In 1928, at the age of seventy-two, Tesla received his last patent, "Apparatus for Aerial Transportation." This was an ingeniously designed flying machine that was a hybrid of a helicopter and airplane. The vehicle would ascend vertically then rotate its engines to fly like an airplane. This was the predecessor of what we now know as the tilt-rotor, or VSTL (Vertical Short Takeoff and Landing), airplane. Today, we know that the VSTL was used regularly in the Gulf War and are regularly used throughout the world.

Tesla IN-VISIONS and Builds the First Electric Car

In 1932, the Pierce-Arrow Automobile Manufacturer and George Westinghouse commissioned Tesla to develop an electric motor to power a car. The motor he built measured a mere forty inches long and thirty inches across, producing about eighty horsepower. The car was tested, reaching speeds of ninety miles per hour.

Under the hood was the engine and a small, twelve-volt storage battery with two thick wires running from the motor to the dashboard. Tesla connected the wires to a small black box, which he had built only weeks before with components he bought from a local radio shop. He didn't allow anyone to inspect the box, but said that it taps into a *"mysterious radiation which comes out of the aether;"* he said that the energy was available free of charge in *"limitless qualities."*

Tesla IN-VISIONS a Death Ray to Save America from German Attack

As Europe marched towards World War II, Tesla invented what the New York Times, front-page headline called a *"Death Beam."* Various sources stated that his device could concentrate beams of particles through the air with such tremendous energy that it could bring down a fleet of ten thousand enemy airplanes at a distance of two hundred and fifty miles, killing entire armies where they stood.

Tesla said that the use of his device would make war unfeasible because it could put an *"Invisible Chinese Wall"* around an entire country. The announcement generated considerable controversy and Tesla was widely criticized as a *"mad scientist"* who was losing his mind.

Frustrated by the lack of interest in his *"Super Weapon to End All Wars,"* Tesla sent detailed schematics of what he *IN-VISIONed* to a number of allied nations, including the United States, Canada, England, France, and the Soviet Union. None were willing to make the investment required to build the device until two years later, when one stage of his plan was tested by the Soviet Union. They sent Tesla a check for twenty-five thousand dollars, but gave little detail of their experiment and had no further communication with him.

**The Man Who IN-VISIONED
More Than Eight Hundred Inventions**

In January of 1943, Tesla died at age eighty-six. He had received more than eight hundred patents in his lifetime and was credited with *"Inventing the Twentieth-Century."*

Upon his death, the United States Government seized all of his experiments, papers, and notebooks, including his treasured black notebook that contained hundreds of pages of technical research notes.

The things that he was developing and on which he was experimenting, including all his papers, were declared top-secret by the War Department, due to the nature of the inventions and patents.

Tesla is Declared the Father of Radio by the Supreme Court

One year later, nearly three decades after Tesla began the fight with Marconi, the U.S. Supreme Court confirmed that Marconi's radio patents indeed infringed on Tesla's patents and inventions; the Court therefore declared that Nikola Tesla was indeed the true "Father of Radio."

Tesla IN-VISIONED Solar Power, Weather Control, Military Defense Systems, Robots, and the Internet

PICTURE PERFECT

In January, 1900, Tesla wrote an article for *Century Magazine*, in which he eagerly described his plans for a future where we could tap into the sun's energy, control the weather with electricity, and end war with machines that would actually make war an impossibility; we could wirelessly transmit power and radio signals around the entire globe, engage in interplanetary communications, and even construct, what he called, robotic "automatons" that would conduct themselves independently of operators, performing difficult chores for industry.

Tesla claimed he could build a *"world system"* of wireless communications to relay telephone signals, news reports, and private messages; the world system would secure military communications and even send pictures to any point in the world.

As a side-note, prior to 1973, mobile phones were limited to those bulky, box-looking units installed in cars and other vehicles. Motorola was the first company to produce a handheld mobile phone. On April 3, 1973, a Motorola researcher and executive made the first mobile telephone call from a handheld subscriber equipment, fulfilling what Tesla had *IN-VISIONed* and predicted seventy-three years earlier.

In 1898, Tesla demonstrated that he could control a boat by remote control and claimed that he could show the Navy how to direct a torpedo using remote control. A year before Wilhelm Rontgen was credited with inventing the X-ray (1895), Tesla had taken and shown a number of X-ray photos to audiences. Although he didn't patent the X-ray device, he was using and demonstrating X-rays before 1895.

Tesla also patented the *AC induction motor (electric motor)* that is commonly used today in household appliances and industry. Obviously, the list of inventions and ideas credited (and uncredited) to Nikola Tesla and their applications may be too numerous to count.

The Sun Shines on the Just and the Unjust

Yet, just as the sun shines on the just and the unjust and both saint and sinner are equally affected by gravity, so, the principle of *IN-VISIONing* will work for anyone who will develop it and work it.

Today, as we think of Tesla and how our lives are benefited by what he *IN-VISIONed* and created, I encourage you to really believe that you also can *IN-VISION* and create amazing new things that will not only benefit your own life, but the lives of many others also.

It is my desire to see Christians everywhere embrace

and understand that the principle of *IN-VISIONing* has been given by God to help us materialize His wonderful promises and create our heart's desires.

"Call on me and I will answer you. I'll tell you marvelous and wondrous things that you could never figure out on your own" (Jeremiah 33:3 MSG).

CHAPTER 19
The Flight Simulator of Your Mind

Throughout this book I have given you many Biblical examples about how when you send yourself the *RIGHT PICTURE*, you can change the outcome of your life. Now I will give you some scientific research and facts that validate the power of *"IN-VISIONing."*

Dr. Charles Garfield, the former NASA researcher and current president of *The Performance-Science Institute* in Berkeley, California, talks about a startling experiment conducted by Soviet sports scientists.

The study examined the effect of mental training, including visualization, on four groups of world-class athletes just prior to the 1980 Olympics in Lake Placid, New York. The four groups of elite athletes were divided as follows:

- Group 1: did 100% physical training, as usual.

- Group 2: did 75% physical training, 25% mental training.

- Group 3: did 50% physical training, 50% mental training.

- Group 4: did 25% physical training, 75% mental training.

What the researchers found was that **Group 4 – the group with the most mental training, the one that included visualization – had shown significantly greater improvement than Group 3!**

Likewise, Group 3 showed more improvement than Group 2, and Group 2 showed more improvement than Group 1. You can understand how these results were astonishing. Who would expect that athletes training mentally would be able to advance further than their counterparts who were training physically?

Dr. Garfield said, *"During mental rehearsal, athletes create MENTAL IMAGES of the exact movements they want to emulate in their sport. Use of this skill substantially increases the effectiveness of their goal-setting, which, up until then, had been little more than a dull listing procedure."*

Denis Waitley, one of America's most respected

authors who has sold over ten million audio programs in fourteen different languages, did similar experiments with Olympic athletes and United States astronauts. His conclusion matched Dr. Garfield's.

Waitley found that when athletes were hooked to sophisticated monitoring equipment, and rehearsed their Olympic event in their mind, that the twitch muscles in their body fired as if they were actually doing the physical event.

By the way, it was Denis Waitley who reminded us, *"You have to have a dream in order to reach your dream."* He also said, *"It's not who you are that holds you back, it's who you think you are not."*

So science has proven that practicing your skill, in your mind, with little physical practice, can produce better results than *ONLY* practicing physically. I have heard stories about individuals in prison, practicing their golf game, only in their mind, and upon being released from prison found their game had actually improved.

If mental exercises and visualization can have such a profound impact on athletes, what kind of impact could it have on you? Why can't you use the same principle of sending yourself powerful new pictures to improve your attitude, confidence, and skills?

Could *IN-VISIONing* impact your learning ability, your golf swing, and your ability to shed weight and stick to a diet? Of course it can!

Have you ever heard the term, "Flight simulator?" The term "Simulate" came into popular use when we learned how the astronauts prepared for their space missions. When they were simulating in the flight simulator, they were actually pre-living the in-space experience, as if it were already happening.

IN-VISIONing gives you the ability to pre-live your dreams and desires in your thought life, as if it were already happening. This process prepares you to receive and experience the real thing.

The First Artificial Heart

The first permanent artificial heart (the Jarvik-7) ever placed into a human being was done so by Dr. William DeVries, in 1982. According to a newspaper report, he said that his philosophy, with respect to surgery, had always been – "Rehearse... rehearse... and then rehearse some more! For if you stick to this principle," he continued, "when it comes time to perform the actual operation, the procedure will have become almost routine for you."

Since the surgery he was to perform had never been done before, the majority of his rehearsal was in his mind. He *IN-VISIONed* what it would be like during the surgery, and he *IN-VISIONed* different scenarios, including complications, that could occur during the surgery and what he would do to solve those problems.

Dr. DeVries is an excellent example of an individual who gave that little bit extra. He took the time and effort to rehearse the operation on the screen of his own mind, *IN-VISIONing* the procedure before he actually performed it in the hospital operating theater.

By taking the extra time and effort to *Visualize* the intricacies of his surgeries, he has become a world renowned surgeon. Because of his accuracy in *IN-VISIONing* the different stages and procedures of the surgery with which he was involved and *IN-VISIONing* the desired outcome, he is destined to be "written up" in the annals of medical history as one of the best surgeons of his time.

What annals of history will you be written up in because you have decided to *IN-VISION* your future?

CHAPTER 20
Living With an Attitude of Gratitude

Many people are curious about why they keep receiving the same kind of unfavorable things over and over again. They are absolutely certain that they are not broadcasting or sending out anything negative, yet in a specific area of their life, negative experiences keep showing up.

This happens because they are broadcasting a negative vibe without even realizing it. The adverse vibe they are sending originates from the feelings that they get from the *Mental Pictures* they develop, copy, and observe on a regular basis.

For example, if you open your wallet or purse and don't see very much money, your observation may give you a feeling of insufficiency, lack, and limitations.

By experiencing the feeling of insufficiency, lack, and limitations, although unintentional, you now begin broadcasting a vibration of lack and insufficiency.

Although you're not doing it on purpose, the Law of Attraction simply responds to the vibe you broadcast from the feelings that your *MENTAL PICTURES* produce. For that reason, it continues to give you more of the same, which is lack, limitations, and insufficiency.

The Law of Attraction doesn't know and doesn't care what's causing you to generate the negative vibration. You might be remembering something, pretending, worrying, thinking about something in a fearful and dreadful way, or, in this case, just observing and making a judgment about what you've observed. In other words, "I don't have much money."

The Law of Attraction doesn't need or care to know *WHY* you are broadcasting negative vibrations; all it does is know that because you broadcasted it – you want it. As you observe the problems, situations, and circumstances with which you are challenged, your observations generate feelings and vibrations that can be either positive or negative. It is these vibrations that place an order for more of the same.

"Positive and negative emotions cannot occupy the mind at the same time. One or the other must dominate. It is your responsibility to make sure that the

positive emotions constitute the dominating influence of your mind." Napoleon Hill

At every moment, you can discover what you have been thinking and the *Mental Pictures* you have been viewing by becoming aware of what or how you are feeling. If you are feeling good, you have been thinking and *Picturing* good things. If you are feeling discouraged or stressed, you have been thinking and *Picturing* discouraging or stressing, harmful things.

At every moment you can tell if the vibration you are sending out is either positive or negative by identifying the corresponding feeling that your thoughts give to you.

The great news is that you can reset your vibration from negative to positive by simply choosing what you wish to *IN-VISION*, then using your will to *IN-VISION* nothing less than God's best.

You can only send out one vibration at a time; thus, when the *Picture* you are looking at changes – the way you feel and your vibration changes also. To reset your vibe, just change the *Picture* at which you are looking, and the thoughts that you are thinking.

The Law of Attraction doesn't remember what vibration you were sending out five minutes ago, five days ago, or five months ago. It is only responding to the vibration you are sending out right now, at this very moment, and it is working to give you more of the same. For that reason, only think about and Picture what you want in all of your *"nows."*

Remember, God told us to *ONLY* think about those things that are lovely and true and of a good report and virtuous and praiseworthy (Philippians 4:8).

Doubts Effect Your Vibration and What You Broadcast

If you doubt whether or not you can have something, you are broadcasting a negative vibration. This negative vibration is diluting or canceling the positive vibration of your desire. Having a strong desire, which corresponds to a positive vibration, and having strong doubts, which correspond to negative vibrations, will cancel each other out.

God said that a double-minded man would not receive anything from the Lord (James 1:7-8). If you are of two opinions about what you can have and do, the faith and the doubt cancel each other out and you receive nothing.

A limiting belief is a repetitive detrimental thought that you think over and over again.

The Most Common Source of Doubt is from Your Own Limiting Beliefs

A limiting belief is usually caused by viewing the wrong kind of *Mental Pictures*. Perhaps you *Picture* yourself failing. Maybe you *Picture* yourself going broke or getting sick. When your thoughts consist of limiting beliefs, you are automatically broadcasting negative vibrations and, before too long, what you have been broadcasting will show up in your life.

If you will apply yourself to personal development and advancing in life, you will be able to identify your limiting beliefs. They are usually found after you say the word "because," as in the phrase, "I can't because..." When you catch yourself saying the word "because," you have just discovered one of your limiting beliefs.

Gratitude

Take time to appreciate things in your life. Take time to appreciate many things and anything. It's the feeling that's attached to your appreciation that's important. Appreciation and gratitude help you offer strong and positive vibrations.

Sometimes, you can find it hard to believe that God

really wants you to have what you desire, even though He said that He does in Psalm 37:4. This is especially true if you're focusing on the fact that you haven't yet reached your goal.

Remember, by concentrating on what you don't have and feeling unhappy, discouraged, and disappointed that you don't have it, you are offering, or broadcasting, into the creative realm around you a negative vibe or vibration.

So instead of thinking, *Picturing*, or saying, "I don't have (whatever it is that you really want)," start thinking, *Picturing*, and saying, "I'm in the process of obtaining (whatever it is you really want)."

Happy thoughts draw happy situations towards you. Jack Canfield; you remember him don't you? He's the guy whose name is on the Chicken Soup for the Soul, books, and who went from only making eight thousand dollars a year to more than one million dollars a year by *VISUALIZING* success. Anyway, he said that he made an agreement with his family to only think about and do those things that are fun and joyful in life.

That's a pretty good philosophy, don't you think?

Poverty is an Abnormal Condition for You

Poverty is an abnormal, artificial condition created by hearing the wrong things, thinking the wrong things, believing the wrong things, speaking the wrong things, and taking the wrong action according to those wrong things.

If poverty exists in your life, it is because you have allowed the wrong *PICTURES* to remain in your mind, continually. Not only have you allowed the wrong pictures to remain in your mind, you have habitually viewed those pictures daily.

Poverty is a condition that is not found in nature. We find that abundance exists everywhere in nature, but poverty only exists in the lives of men who *IN-VISION* incorrectly. Since the only way to effectively change the external conditions is to improve the internal conditions, flip the script!

You do that by *IN-VISIONing* abundance!

Since lack and insufficiency do not exist in God or in nature, why should it exist for you? It shouldn't!

For that reason, begin at once to *PICTURE PERFECT PROSPERITY!*

CHAPTER 21
Lincoln Logs & Legos

In order to see how *IN-VISION* works in real life, let's consider the story of God's promise to Abraham and Sarah about having a baby.

Genesis 18:1-15 NIV

1 The LORD appeared to Abraham near the great trees of Mamre while he was sitting at the entrance to his tent in the heat of the day. 2 Abraham looked up and saw three men standing nearby. When he saw them, he hurried from the entrance of his tent to meet them and bowed low to the ground. 3 He said, "If I have found favor in your eyes, my lord, do not pass your servant by. 4 Let a little water be brought, and then you may all wash your feet and rest under this tree. 5 Let me get you something to eat, so you can be refreshed and then go on your way—now that you have come to your servant." "Very well," they answered, "do as you say."

6 So Abraham hurried into the tent to Sarah. "Quick," he said, "get three measures of fine flour and knead it and bake some bread." 7 Then he ran to the herd and selected a choice, tender calf and gave it to a servant, who hurried to prepare it. 8 He then brought some curds and milk and the calf that had been prepared, and set these before them. While they ate, he stood near them under a tree.

9 "Where is your wife Sarah?" they asked him. "There, in the tent," he said. 10 Then the LORD said, "I will surely return to you about this time next year, and Sarah your wife will have a son." Now Sarah was listening at the entrance to the tent, which was behind him

11 Abraham and Sarah were already old and well advanced in years, and Sarah was far past the age of childbearing. 12 So Sarah laughed to herself as she thought, "After I am worn out and old, and my master is old, will I now have the pleasure of having a child?"

13 Then the LORD said to Abraham, "Why did Sarah laugh and say, 'Will I really have a child, now that I am old?' 14 Is anything too hard for the LORD? I will return to you at the appointed time next year and Sarah

will have a son."

15 Sarah was afraid, so she lied and said, "I did not laugh." But he said, "Yes, you did laugh."

Too Good to Be True

When Sarah first heard that God said she would have a child, she laughed. The reason she laughed was because she was one hundred percent sure that what God had said was unscientific, unreasonable, impossible, and flat-out ridiculous. It was way too hard to even imagine that what God said would be true, especially for her. She could only *IN-VISION* dying childless.

She immediately thought of all the logical reasons why she couldn't bear children:

1. She knew scientifically that she was past childbearing age.

2. She knew she had stopped having her menstrual cycle many years earlier.

3. She knew she was an old woman and that Abraham was an old man.

4. She had never even heard of anyone close to

her age having a baby.

Overwhelming *EVIDENCE* confirmed that what God said… couldn't happen. In her thinking, it was ridiculous to even entertain the thought of having a baby; the statement made by God was so absurd and so far-fetched, that it made her laugh.

Do you have your own mental list, like Sarah did, of things that have been drilled into you, things that you've accepted about *who you are, what you can become, have, and do*, or things that are so ridiculous today that they are laughable?

Although the notion of having a baby seemed too good to be true, later, she did, in fact, have a baby. Hebrews 11:11 tells us how the seemingly impossible, became possible. *"By faith Sarah also herself received strength to become pregnant, and delivered a child when she was past age, because she judged Him faithful who had made the promise."*

Notice the statement: *"By Faith."* Faith is a spiritual commodity that you acquire by associating with God, His Word, and His Promises. And it's *BY FAITH* that what you desire is going to happen for you, also. After Hebrews 11:11 says, *"By Faith,"* it says, *"She judged Him faithful who promised."*

Every day you pass judgment on God; actually, you

judge Him multiple times each day. You get His Help depending on whether you judge your circumstances, limiting beliefs, and previous experiences faithful — or whether you judge God faithful.

What happened between the time Sarah heard the promise and laughed and the day she actually delivered a baby? Since God is no respecter of persons, if we can discover what Sarah did, we will be able to copy that process and get results for things that today seem impossible to us.

Remember: *"God is no respecter of persons"* means that when anyone creates the same cause, they can get the same desirable effect or results.

Example: Once you learn how to build a cool fort for your kids or grandkids out of Lincoln Logs or Legos, you can repeat the process and get the same results again and again.

Before we look at what Sarah did that materialized for her what at first seemed ridiculous, let's look at a modern example of what is considered ridiculous to most people.

People Magazine

In 2007, the day after *The Oscars*, the *People Magazine* website had 51.7 million page-views from Americans who wanted to know who won what awards at *The Oscars* and what their favorite celebrities were wearing and saying.

Every week, *People Magazine* sells several million issues of their magazine, featuring the lifestyles of popular celebrities. Americans who are infatuated with *Rich and Famous* celebrities seem to be obsessed with learning about the restaurants at which they eat, the brand of clothes they wear, what kind of cars they drive, where they vacation, what their houses look like, their likes, their dislikes, etc.

The millions of Americans who follow the lives and lifestyles of the Rich and Famous never imagine or *IN-VISION* that they themselves could eat at the same restaurants, wear similar clothes, drive the same kind of cars, and vacation where the rich and famous vacation. Like Sarah, to even imagine these things for themselves would make them laugh.

For that reason, they live vicariously through the people they admire, never imagining or *IN-VISIONing* that they could have an even more wonderful, happy, and fulfilling life and experience than their favorite celebrities.

Imagination is Real – Treat it as Such

Sarah had to get to the place that she *imagined* and *IN-VISIONed* herself with a child. She had to send herself *mental pictures* of her with her baby. For some reason, we falsely think that our imagination is not real. We have a tendency to think that an imagination is like a fairytale or a vapor of smoke.

Everything formed and created that you use and see daily started as an imagination. *Imagination* is behind every good idea; imagination is how the good idea was materialized. Someone had to *IN-VISION* it before it could be created. If imagination were not real, then every created thing around you would vanish instantly and you would be standing naked in the desert or in the mountains because everything around you started in the imagination of someone.

Hold your hands out in front of you about a foot apart. What's in-between your hands? It's *AIR*. Now, in that space, hold a purse, iPad, bottle of water, or another object. First, there was just air, then there was something. What made the something? *IMAGINATION*.

IN-VISIONing what you Imagine as real and tangible is the beginning process of the creative power of God in you.

Fifteen Principles Explaining How IN-VISION Works

1. You must form a clear and definite *mental picture* of what you want. To start the creative process, you cannot be vague about what you want or desire.

2. You must send yourself a clear mental picture of what you want to become or have and imagine it as you wish it to look when you get it. Send yourself a clear *Mental Picture* of confidence, poise, prosperity, favor, or of obtaining and experiencing certain desirable things.

3. As a ship's captain has in mind the port towards which he is sailing his ship, you must keep your face toward what you have *IN-VISIONed* at all times. You must no more lose sight of your mental picture or vision than the ship's navigator loses sight of his compass.

4. Believe that the more clear and definite you make your picture and the more you imagine it, bringing out all its delightful details, the stronger your desire, creativity, and attraction for what you desire will be.

5. Behind your clear vision must be the real intention to actually realize it and to bring it into

tangible expression so that you and others can experience it.

6. Don't allow yourself to be satisfied only seeing someone else doing or having what you want to do and have. *That's the voyeurism of the People Magazine mentality.* You must actually want to experience it for yourself and be determined that you will experience it.

   The process begins like this: at first, when you see something desirable you may say, *"I could never have something that nice."* That's kind of what Sarah did. Having a child was for someone else, but not her. As you keep what you desire before your eyes, you soon end up saying things like *"That would sure be nice to have"* or *"I wish I could have something like that."*

   Yet, the more you hold fast to your *IN-VISION*, or Imagination, and add vivid details, you will soon say, *"I WILL someday have or be that!"* After steadfastly holding onto your vision with the intention of actually experiencing it, you will someday say, *"That's mine!"* Do you see the progression?

7. The whole thing turns on receiving. Behind your intention of actually realizing what you desire, must be an invincible and unwavering faith that

the thing is already yours, just as you have *IN-VISIONed* or *pictured* it.

That's the whole meaning of what Jesus said in Mark 11:24. He said, *"Whatever you ask for in prayer, believe that you received it, and you shall have it."*

8. We must ask, believing that what we've asked for has been granted and is already ours, before we can actually possess what we have asked of God.

9. Contemplate your vision until it is clear and distinct; then, take the mental attitude of owning everything in the *picture* and, at the same time, be sure to act on any opportunities that are presented to you that will get you closer to your vision.

10. In your imagination, start enjoying the things you desire. Take possession of it all in your mind, in full faith that it actually belongs to you now because God, your heavenly Father, has granted it to you as He said He would.

Hold the mental ownership for what you ask of God. Let me explain. Live in the new house, mentally, until it takes form around you, physically. See the things you desire as if they were actually around you all the time. See yourself owning, using, and experiencing them. Make use of them in your imagination just as you will use them when they are your tangible possessions. Thank God for the lovely environment and things you desire before you experience them, physically.

The bride to be imagines her fairy tale wedding, even down to the last detail. In her *IN-VISIONing*, she *SEES* both the tangible and intangible. In her mind, she sees the colors she wants to use, she sees the stemware, the linens, the flowers, the food, the table settings, and she sees all her family and friends in attendance. These are the tangible things she *IN-VISIONs*.

However, she also *SEES* the intangible. She sees the approval in her parents' faces and the delight of her friends as she walks down the aisle. She can also *IN-VISION* the love her groom expresses as he sees her for the first time in her wedding gown and she can clearly see this day being filled with joy, happiness, wonderful memories, and love.

11. Be as thankful for what you *IN-VISION*, what you desire, and what you asked for as you expect to be when it has actually materialized. Those who

can sincerely thank God for the thing that they own only in their imagination have real faith and will receive exactly what they've asked of Him.

12. Once you have clearly formed in your imagination the thing you desire, your success depends on receiving it. You must, in your mind, receive what you ask for. Imagine it. *IN-VISION* it. Receive it.

13. Think and speak of all the things for which you ask *"AS IF"* you already actually owned them. You must *OWN* those things in your thinking before you can experience them. Your *IN-VISION*, or *INNER-Vision*, is part of your faith and belief system. It is your *IN-VISION* that is the connection between *"WHAT CAN BE"* and *"WHAT CURRENTLY IS."* It joins the Invisible to the Visible. It bridges the gap between the Promised and the Manifested.

14. Improve and increase the capacity of your Imagination. Start imagining your environment, finances, and relationships exactly as you want them. Live all the time in the mental environment that those things are yours already, having faith that God is getting involved and causing the actual creation of what you Picture.

15. Hold the faith that what you have embraced

and *IN-VISIONed* is now being realized and hold fast to your intention to experience it. Remember that faith and intention in the use of your imagination are what makes the difference between the receiver and the dreamer.

How to Receive - in a Nutshell

Many people fail to communicate to God what they really want because they only have a vague and misty idea of the things they want to do, have, or become. These people say things like, "I want my life to be better," or "I just want to be happy," or "I just want some more money." They cannot state in definite terms what "better," "happy," or "more" really mean; nor can they discuss what they really want. They have a foggy, blurred, and distorted *Mental Picture.*

Behind your clear vision, desire, or imagination must be the real intention to realize it, to bring it into tangible expression, and to really have it. Without this real intention, your thoughts, words, and actions won't correspond with what you have *IN-VISIONed.*

By thinking about what you desire and finding scriptures that promise you what you desire, you will develop an invincible and unwavering faith that you already have what you desire.

You must, in your mind, with all your might, and by using your imagination, receive what you asked God for, and live in the spirit of owning the things you *IN-VISION* and believe you have received.

CHAPTER 22
Einstein Explains Hebrews 11

"Through faith we understand that the worlds were framed by the word of God, so that the things which are seen were not made of things that do appear" *(Hebrews 11:3).*

God framed (or created) the worlds (planets, stars, galaxies, and our solar system) with His Words. God spoke what He *IN-VISIONed* but could not be seen – then what He *IN-VISIONed* became seen. That which He *IN-VISIONed* was intangible, but became material.

Maybe the things you desire, such as happiness, peace, prosperity, great relationships, and blessings of every kind can't be seen in your tangible world. They are not what you are currently experiencing. However, like God, begin to *IN-VISION* and speak those things, just the way you want them to be, and they shall become.

Since you are made in the image of God, God wants you to create your world with what you *IN-VISION* and with your words, just as He did in the beginning, as recorded in Genesis 1, and Hebrews 11:3.

If you do not like the world you have previously created for yourself with words of discord, lack, limitation, and hard times, you can begin building a new world of limitless good and prosperity by changing the *PICTURES* you send to yourself and the words you speak and decree.

God gave us words and the ability to paint *Word Pictures* of what we want in life. *"You shall also decree a thing and it shall be established unto you"* (Job 22:28).

Isaiah 10:1 says, *"Woe to them that decree unrighteous decrees."* I take that to mean that you will experience woeful situations if you decree or talk fear, doubt, unbelief, problems, difficulties, and any other thing you don't want to experience.

The Law of Command is one of the easiest and fastest ways to produce rich results. You simply command or decree what you desire; similar to the way that God created the universe, and it happens. However, there is a catch.

You must first really *IN-VISION* what you want to happen before your command or decree will have the power to produce desirable results.

"Through faith we understand that the worlds were framed by the word of God, so that the things which are seen were not made of things that do appear" (Hebrews 11:3). God framed the world and every living thing with words derived from what He wanted and *VISUALIZED*.

You are the sculptor and creator of your world. You sculpt and create your world using the words that you speak, which are based upon the Mental Pictures you send yourself (or others have sent you) and view on a regular basis.

Generally speaking, what you talk about all day long is based on your inner image of yourself, others, situations, circumstances, and the activities that are happening around you.

When you catch yourself complaining and saying words such as "lack," "limitation," "unlucky," or "great things can't happen for me" and so forth, it is a clue that you have been viewing those kinds of *Mental Photographs,* perhaps without even being aware of it.

Look at it like this: whatever words you've been speaking are a direct giveaway of the type of *Pictures* you've been mentally viewing for some time.

Now that you've been made aware of the principle that words are connected to what you have been thinking and *Picturing*, you can identify what you've been *Picturing* and begin to change what you've been getting by creating a *Perfect Picture* of a new and better life!

Jesus said, *"Out of the abundance of your heart (mind), your mouth will speak"* (Matthew 12:34). If you catch yourself speaking negative or unwanted things, Jesus said that the reason you are doing this is because you have been thinking or *Picturing* negative and unwanted things.

As you know, when you think and speak negative and unwanted things, that's what shows up in your life. This explains very simply and clearly how you've come to have what you never wanted.

Forget the Form, Ceremony, and Ritual Give Me Something that Really Works!

I personally know many pastors who can talk at length about the theory and concept of successful living, but, unfortunately, they are demonstrating very little of it. They are big on advice, but small on results. They have not yet grasped the fact that what they

PICTURE in their mind and think about is a crucial part of receiving from God.

The masses today are lonely – lonely for a spiritual, victorious way of life that isn't just filled with man-made theory and doctrines about rule-keeping and behavior modification, but one that really works and produces health, peace, happiness, and abundance in their lives.

You can have any of God's rich blessings if you are willing to pay the price. I'm not talking about a works-trip, trying to do things to gain favor with God or earn blessings from God, but about daily affirming and *Purposefully Picturing* what you desire.

You, indeed, become what you desire to be, by *Picturing* and affirming what you desire to be, and eventually getting to the place that you can *SEE* yourself as already being what you desire to be.

It is a good idea to write out whatever you desire and really wish to experience. It's also important to read those notes about your desires and to read them frequently. By doing this you will begin to *Picture Perfectly* what you desire. As you do this, *mentally imagine* and *Picture* successful results. Finally, boldly and deliberately affirm, decree, and command those successful results to appear.

The process looks like this: first you think about what you want and desire. You then begin to formulate *Pictures* of your desire. As a result, what you've *Pictured* in your mind should lead you to clearly write down, in detail, your desire. Following this process will only lead you to more clarity about what you want in this life.

Now, we start doing what Jesus spoke of in Matthew 12:34: your mouth automatically gives voice to what has now become a *Perfect Picture* in your heart and mind! Out of the abundance of your heart your mouth now speaks! If you persist in this daily practice, nothing will be able to stop the flood tide of blessing that will start overflowing your life.

The Laws of Increase

"The LORD shall increase you more and more, you and your children. You are blessed of the LORD which made heaven and earth" (Psalm 115:14-15). Since this verse tells you that the will of God is to increase you, you should think thoughts and speak words that are in line with the prosperity and increase that God wants for your life; do it boldly and positively.

You should at all times imagine and *IN-VISION* God's

laws of increase working for you. You should think about and write notes about how God is increasing you. The act of writing out your goals, desires, and those things for which you are grateful imprints those things indelibly on your mind, improving the definition of your *Picture*, which is the goal.

What will *"increase and multiplication"* look like to you? What will it feel like to experience the increase and multiplication of God in your life? Think about and Mentally Picture increase and multiplication; let yourself experience the feeling of increase, all day long.

The God in Heaven, He Will Prosper Our Way

In the Bible, it was Nehemiah who used the *Law of Increase* to get the destroyed walls of Jerusalem rebuilt after the Jews returned from captivity in Babylon. Nehemiah had favor on his life while he was a simple servant of the king. By utilizing God's favor on his life, he was able to secure materials and manpower from the King to rebuild the walls of Jerusalem.

He soon discovered that hostile tribes had occupied Jerusalem while the Jews were in exile. It was necessary for Nehemiah to organize two crews of workmen: one crew to build the walls of Jerusalem and one crew to guard against the enemy tribes.

Nehemiah had an affirmation that he had to frequently think, *IN-VISION*, and decree. He said, *"The God of heaven, He will prosper our way"* (Nehemiah 2:20).

You should take a moment now to speak those inspired words with boldness and confidence:

"The God in Heaven – He Will Prosper My Way!"

Read it again, but this time declare it boldly, out loud, so that you hear yourself telling you what God wants you to believe and experience! Now, take an additional moment and send yourself a *Picture* of what God prospering your way will look like. That's how it's done.

Joshua and Caleb IN-VISIONed Victory

Perhaps Joshua and Caleb are two of the most prosperous thinkers in the Bible. Of the twelve leaders whom Moses sent to inspect the Promised Land to verify its excellence, Joshua and Caleb were the only two leaders who *IN-VISIONed* the possibility of them actually possessing and experiencing what God had graciously provided for them and commanded them to possess.

The ten other popular leaders reported that the land was rich, just like God said it was. However, they focused and thought more about the giants in the land than the promise that God had given them.

The thinking of the majority was that it would be suicide to even attempt to have what God said they could have. Although they said, "there's no way," Joshua and Caleb confidently declared, *"Let us go up at once and possess it; for we are well able to overcome the giants and take the land"* (Numbers 13:30).

Everyone was against the plan of possessing what God had given to them. They were incapable of *Picturing* themselves having the very best that God and the world had to offer. For that reason, the Children of Israel remained in the wilderness, experiencing a lack-luster and boring existence until they died there. Only after their death did their children get to enter into and possess the best land in the world.

God has a plan for you to possess the abundance He has provided for you, but you must cooperate with His plan by implementing the principles I'm giving you in this book.

Years later, when the children of those who were

present when the spies were sent finally did go into the Promised Land, they discovered that there were very few giants, even though the previous report given to their parents was that *ALL* the people in the land were giants.

Because of their hesitation to go into the land and claim their God-given blessings, their parents only prolonged their stay in the misery of the wilderness and died there. Eventually, their children had to face the situation and master its challenges anyway. The same applies to each of us.

Many Christians unknowingly use the *Law of Decrease* instead of the *Law of Increase* and limit their opportunities and blessings. For this reason, they find that they are never quite satisfied with the limited results they are experiencing. Perhaps their needs are met, but they know in their heart that there is more available, yet just out of reach.

If you want more out of life, you have to begin applying the Laws of Increase that God put in His Word. So why not do it starting now and move into the Promised Land rather than remaining in the wilderness of want, lack, and discouragement? It all begins with you trashing the *Mental Pictures* that insist that things must remain as they've always been and start creating new, powerful, and exciting *Mind Pictures*.

Transubstantiation

God's desire for us is that we take His Word of promise off the pages of our Bible and get those promises real and materialized in our lives. God wants what He paid for. This means that He wants us to have and experience what Jesus died to obtain for us. God wants us to take what we need out of the spiritual realm and get it real in the physical realm where we can use it.

We are discovering that focused thought and imagination enable us to *transcend the physical world and its obvious limitations* and create from the spirit world what we imagine and *IN-VISION*. Remember that God created the things that we see from things that cannot be seen (Hebrews 11:3). The things that could not be seen, but were still real, were *transubstantiated* into things that can be seen, and now are real.

Transubstantiation basically means to change from one substance into another. According to the Council of Trent, the Catholic Church believes that when prayer is made over the holy sacraments of communion (the Eucharist), the bread and the wine change *substance* and actually become the physical body and blood of Jesus Christ. This change in substance is called *transubstantiation*.

Protestants believe that the bread and wine always remain bread and wine; they only *REPRESENT* the body and blood of Jesus Christ. Protestants believe that our partaking of communion is to remember what Jesus did for us through His broken body (which purchased healing for our bodies) and shed blood (which purchased forgiveness of our sins).

Einstein's Scientific Explanation for Hebrews 11:3

Albert Einstein shook up the scientific world when he claimed that substance and matter are convertible (can be transubstantiated). He declared that the formed (what we would call physical matter) and unformed world (the invisible world around us that we might call the spiritual realm) are made out of the same energy, ether, or substance. He said that the visible and invisible realms are relative, convertible, and interchangeable.

He was saying, in effect, that that which is invisible can become material. As Christians, we would describe this by saying that the things of the spiritual realm can become our physical experience.

We know without a doubt *"that the worlds were made by the Word of God, so that the things which* are seen were not made of things which can be seen" (Hebrews 11:3). The physical and material world, that at one time didn't even exist, was made by the spiritual world that always existed.

God said that our faith is the substance of the things we hope for (Hebrews 11:1). Stated another way, *"Our faith gives substance and tangibility to the things that at one time we merely hoped for, and were invisible,"* *"Our faith takes that which is invisible and causes it to change substance from the invisible realm to the visible realm,"* or *"Our faith takes from the supply that is real in the creative or spiritual realm of God, and causes it to materialize in our physical world, so we can benefit from it."*

From a standpoint of *IN-VISIONing* your heart's desires, we can then blend Hebrews 11:1 with Einstein's theory that the invisible can be converted into the visible.

If the formed and unformed worlds are connected and relative, then you have nothing to worry about if your finances ever get low. You can use what Einstein described as a law of relativity to *IN-VISION*, thus, produce either money or its financial equivalent to meet your needs.

CHAPTER 23
God's Businessman

I want to share with you a story about a famous Christian millionaire and inventor of heavy earthmoving machinery. His name was R.G. LeTourneau (1888 – 1969).

In the days in which we live, nearly everyone has heard about Bill Gates and Steve Jobs; these men are certainly responsible for helping to change our world in an exciting way. But I've got to say that I get even more excited as I research Christian men and women who have succeeded in a big financial way and how they have helped change our world.

The great thing is that in the process of growing their businesses and accumulating wealth, these wonderful Christians glorified God and had the will and ability to donate millions of dollars to promote the Gospel and bless worthwhile charities. These are the kind of role models that we believers need to know more about and, certainly, LeTourneau was one of these amazing men of God.

I first heard about this mighty man twenty or more years ago. I was told that God would give him an idea, a vision, or a dream and he would meditate on what God was showing him, trying to *IN-VISION* what God was communicating. I had heard that, at times, he would draw what he was *IN-VISIONing* on a napkin and give the drawing to his engineers, instructing them to create what he had drawn.

Usually, they told him that his ideas couldn't possibly work and that he shouldn't waste the time or money trying to develop what he was *VISUALIZING*. Yet, as LeTourneau insisted that what he had drawn would work, the engineers created electric motors, gears and transmissions, and other things from his drawings that did work and they revolutionized earthmoving equipment across the entire world.

What He IN-VISIONed Made Him Millions and Helped Win the War

I was surprised to discover that LeTourneau's

machines represented nearly seventy percent of the earthmoving equipment and engineering vehicles used during World War II.

Over the course of his life he secured nearly three hundred patents.

He and his wife founded LeTourneau University, a private, Christian institution in Longview, Texas. LeTourneau was widely known as a devoted Christian, and a generous philanthropist to Christian causes.

God's Businessman

LeTourneau's contemporaries respectfully referred to him as "God's businessman," because he gave God the glory for the things he first *IN-VISIONed* and later invented.

Traditional education held little interest for LeTourneau; in 1902, at the age of fourteen, he left school with the blessing, but concern, of his Christian parents. He learned the foundry and machinist trades while on the job and studied mechanics from an International Correspondence School course that had been given to him, even though he never completed any of the course assignments.

He later moved to San Francisco, where he worked at the Yerba Buena Power Plant, learned welding, and became familiar with the application of electricity. He was rejected for military service because of neck injuries sustained in a race car crash. But in May 1921, he *IN-VISIONed* a great plant where he would create earthmoving equipment. He believed God and purchased a plot of land in Stockton and established an engineering workshop, where he designed and built several types of scrapers and made improvements on earthmoving equipment.

LeTourneau Gains Worldwide Fame

LeTourneau completed many earthmoving projects during the 1920s and early 1930s, including the Boulder Highway to the Hoover Dam, in Nevada, the Marysville Levees, the Orange County Dam, and the Newhall Cut-off in California. The LeTourneau name became synonymous with earthmoving, worldwide.

LeTourneau was largely responsible for the invention and development of many types of earthmoving machines now widely used today. (It's common for us to simply refer to them as Caterpillars). His use of the *IN-VISION* Principle enabled him to literally view and influence the future. My desire is that the *IN-*

VISION Principle will enable you to view, influence, and customize your future, as you desire and as God intends.

LeTourneau designed and built machines using technology that was years, sometimes decades, ahead of its time and became recognized worldwide as a leader in the development and manufacture of heavy equipment.

What he *IN-VISIONed* was years ahead of its time, but not ahead of God. God has some amazing things that He wants to release into the world that will help the world immensely. The only thing is, He needs someone to *IN-VISION* what can be and then seek His guidance on how to bring it about.

Some of LeTourneau's Accomplishments Include...

The use of rubber tires in earthmoving, numerous improvements relating to scrapers, the development of low-pressure, heavy-duty rubber tires, the two-wheeled tractor unit (called the, "Tournapull"), electric wheel drive, and mobile offshore drilling platforms: all are attributed to LeTourneau's ingenuity.

As previously discussed, during his lifetime, LeTourneau generated and gave away millions of dollars to Christian projects and charities. I know that I *IN-VISION* myself giving away large sums of money to promote the Gospel. I *IN-VISION* people being saved, delivered, redeemed, fulfilled, and so much more because of my giving. I also *IN-VISION* families being reunited and people once again having a purpose for their lives because of the contributions I make to promote the Gospel of Jesus Christ. I encourage you to start *IN-VISIONing* yourself doing the same.

LeTourneau Finally Gets a Diploma

LeTourneau increased with the increase of God! He soon offered contractors a range of high capacity earthmoving and material handling machines. These were all based on the revolutionary electric wheel drive system that God had shown him and that he had *IN-VISIONed*. He also developed an electric wheel drive called an "Electric Wheel Hub Motor."

In 1965, the International Correspondence School awarded LeTourneau his diploma in engineering, fifty years after he initially studied the course. LeTourneau was seventy-six at the time and, upon accepting the diploma, joyfully remarked to an executive assistant, "So now I've got a diploma. Now I'm educated."

LeTourneau held many respected positions throughout his life as a Christian layman, including leader in the Christian & Missionary Alliance Church, president of the Christian Business Men's Committee (CBMC), and president of the Gideons International (you know, the ministry that puts Bibles into hotel rooms).

LeTourneau Seeds his Wisdom into Others

Being a man of great Christian commitment and dedication for thirty years, he flew thousands of miles each week to maintain Christian speaking engagements around the United States and overseas, seeding his wisdom and insight into others in an effort to help them succeed and prosper.

In 1946, he purchased an unused military hospital and its accompanying land and buildings in Longview, Texas. There he established the LeTourneau Technical Institute at the site of the former Harmon General Hospital to provide sound technical and mechanical training, traditional college courses, and training for missionary technicians based on the philosophy of combining work, education, and Christian testimony.

His desire was to send mechanically trained workers

into Third World countries to help them develop as they shared the gospel with the locals.

The LeTourneau Technical Institute became a college in its own right. In 1961, it eventually gained "University" status to become LeTourneau University. Today, the University is a busy and growing institution, offering degrees in engineering, aeronautical sciences, and liberal arts, along with a strong Christian influence including three times weekly compulsory chapel attendance for students.

George H. Atkinson, of the highly respected U.S. Contractors, Guy F. Atkinson Company, of San Francisco, said, "There is hardly any place in the vast industry that has not benefited through the products of Mr. LeTourneau's inventive genius." Part of LeTourneau's genius was his ability to get quiet before God and *IN-VISION* what others could not.

LeTourneau's World Vision and Outreach

In 1953, LeTourneau began a development project in the country of Liberia, West Africa, with the diverse goals of colonization, land development, agricultural development, livestock introduction, evangelism, and Christian charity work. In 1954, a colonization project with similar objectives to those in Liberia had already been established in the country of Peru, South America, leading to thousands of salvations.

I want you to use your *sanctified imagination* and start *IN-VISIONing* the wonderful things that can be accomplished with great sums of money. Then I want you to *IN-VISION* the wonderful things you will be able to do for others as God delivers into your hands wealth and riches.

The world's fields are ripe with a great harvest of souls. It will require a vast amount of wealth to reap the harvest. God has raised you up for such a time as this. So get comfortable with the thought of being rich. Do not only *IN-VISION* having *YOUR* every need met, but also, start to *IN-VISION* having enough to help meet the needs of others.

CHAPTER 24
The Super Bowl of Your Life!

For the first time in many years, I watched several N.F.L. football games in 2013. Up until the 2013 season, I exclusively only enjoyed watching college football and not professional football. In 2013, I had a blast watching the amazing athleticism of the pros.

On Sunday, February 2, 2014, I had the pleasure of watching Super Bowl XLVIII, with my sons. Because of my new fondness for the pros, a few weeks after the big game, I researched some random information about the Super Bowl. I found some interesting statistics and, particularly, one thing pertaining to *IN-VISIONing* that I want to share with you.

The information I read said that there were approximately seventy TV cameras videoing the events on and off the field, during the game. That got me thinking. At least seventy cameras are capturing and sending images to a studio somewhere in the stadium or in a studio trailer out in the parking lot. In the studio is a director watching, possibly, up to seventy video monitors at the same time and making decisions, on the fly, as to which image will go live across America and around the world.

Obviously, we viewers only get to see one camera feed at a time, unless the director decides to show us a split-screen containing several camera feeds at a time. Then we would get to see the split-screen through the eyes of two or more cameras. Think about it.

- Some of the cameras are sending video images of individual players.

- Some of the cameras are sending images of different coaches, trying to capture their reaction to certain plays or calls by the referee.

- Some cameras show different angles of the action on the field, or maybe even an aerial view from the blimp.

- Some cameras send images of cheerleaders.

- Some cameras send images of the crowd holding up clever signs with slogans about their team or their favorite player.

- Some of the cameras send images that are totally unrelated to football.

- Some of the cameras capture and send images of the pretty women in the crowd, children with their faces painted, and guys all dressed up in their team colors, wearing outrageous costumes.

- Some of the cameras send blurry images of the grass, cables, or other unintelligible images because the cameraman is on the move, changing positions while the camera pans random images very rapidly.

- Some cameras are sending images that are sideways because the cameraman is on break and has laid the camera down at a tilted angle.

- Some cameras might even show some guy's rear end because he may have inadvertently walked in front of the camera.

In addition to the overwhelming amount of images on the seventy monitors, there are also additional monitors that have commercials queued up; the directors must show these regularly throughout the game. Talk about a high stress job.

The director in the studio is inundated with video *PICTURES*, and must decide in a fraction of a second whether to show the world what he or she is seeing on Monitor 5, Monitor 32, Monitor 24, Monitor 59, Monitor 47, etc., or whether to now cut to a commercial.

Remember, the director must instantly decide between Camera Feed 1 and Camera Feed 70 what the world will see. As he or she calls out the number to the technician doing the switching, whatever number video feed the director selects, is what *WE* see.

You are Like the Video Director for the Super Bowl

YOU are kind of like the video director of the Super Bowl in that you are the one responsible for the *IMAGE* that gets played on the screen of your mind. At any given moment, there may be *HUNDREDS* of video images being fed in to the monitors of your mind. *YOU* must choose which *PICTURE* gets played and watched on the big screen of your mind.

What if the Video Director Goes Crazy?

Hypothetically, what if the video director at the Super Bowl locked the studio doors and sabotaged the program by only showing the world the weird images that some of the cameras were capturing, and not showing anything pertaining to the game? When you get sixty to ninety thousand people in one place, strange and inappropriate things can happen that wouldn't be good for the public, especially the children, to see.

It's not my intention to gross you out, but let's get real here. Let's imagine the bizarre things that might get captured by a roving camera.

- A camera might capture an exhausted player puking.

- We might see and hear players and coaches cussing one another out.

- We might see drunk college guys mooning the camera for fun.

- A football player might hide around a circle of players, or among some equipment, urinating in the grass along the sidelines.

- We might see rowdy people starting fights in the crowd or a section of people passing around bottles of whiskey or joints.

Certainly those and similar images are captured and sent into the editing studio during every game, but we don't see those things because the N.F.L., F.C.C., and television network has ordered the director to only select and broadcast images that are fun, wholesome, and pertaining to football.

However, in the 2004 Super Bowl game, during the fabulous halftime extravaganza, there was a *wardrobe malfunction* involving Janet Jackson that broadcasted around the world. The network received a reprimand and a large fine from the F.C.C. and the National Football League had to make official statements about their commitment to family entertainment. The objectionable video images were viewed, and the controversy regarding this matter was discussed for weeks.

The point is that *YOU* are the director and at any given time there are many strange and inappropriate *PICTURES* flooding into your mind. What you choose to do with those *pictures* determines how big and wonderful, or how small and petty, your life will turn out.

Every day that you continue viewing the unwholesome *pictures* of failure, misfortune, betrayal, and bitterness of your past, becomes another day that you drag your past disappointing results into your future.

It's Time For Something New and Exciting!

This is the day that the Lord has made. I will rejoice and be glad in it by sending myself new and powerful *MENTAL IMAGES* of who I am, now that I am *IN-CHRIST.*

Every day should be a new creation full of possibilities and opportunities, not a repeat of the past, containing the lack and struggle that you disdain.

With all of my heart, I want you to win in life. With all of my heart, I am persuaded that if you will embrace and faithfully practice the principles I have given you in this book, your life will be amazing in the days ahead.

So keep receiving from God by sending yourself, and viewing, *PICTURES* of what God has promised and of what you desire.

God bless you richly, Pastor Rob

About Pastor Rob

Pastor Rob Spina is the Founding Pastor of Hope Unlimited Church in Monrovia, California.

He is the recipient of numerous awards including the "Champion of Destiny" award for building fresh water wells in third world countries.

Pastor Rob is a life long student of the Word and has earned his Doctorate of Ministry Degree.

With more than 35 years in ministry, he is committed to bringing the Good News of Jesus Christ and His grace to hurting people outside the church walls, through Television, the Internet, Books, CDs, and Seminars.

Pastor Rob has seen supernatural growth in his church and ministry over the past couple of years and is aggressively providing ministry, resources, and encouragement to fellow Pastors, helping them to fulfill their calling and destiny.

He is the author of several books, including Breakdown or Breakthrough, The Wisdom of James, Changing Your Life by Changing the Way You Think, and Better Days Ahead.

Pastor Rob has a daily television program in the Philippines and you can watch his Live-Stream or past video messages at www.thehopeuc.com

Pastor Rob is a bold and dynamic teacher and preacher, with a great sense of humor, who loves to incorporate mind challenging illustrations and videos into his messages that will dare you to live on Monday what you learned on Sunday.

To find out more, please visit *www.thehopeuc.com*